ILLUSTRATED CATALOGUE

OF

STANDARD GAUGE LOCOMOTIVES

MANUFACTURED BY

THE DICKSON MANUFACTURING CO.

Illustrated Catalogue

OF

Standard Gauge Locomotives

MANUFACTURED BY

The Dickson Manufacturing Company

SCRANTON, PA.

AND

112 LIBERTY STREET, NEW YORK CITY,

U. S. A.

H. M. BOIES, *President.*

JAMES P. DICKSON, *Vice-President.*   W. H. PERKINS, *Secretary and Treasurer.*

JOHN DEVINE, *Sup't Locomotive Works.*

SIDNEY BROADBENT, *Sup't Penn Avenue Works.*   JOHN M. DANIELS, *Sup't Wilkes-Barre Works.*
E. K. SANCTON, *Ass't "   "   "*   GEO. W. WATTS, *Mechanical Engineer.*

E. D. LEAVITT, JR., *D. M. E., Consulting Engineer.*

GEO. B. ROSS, *Agent in New York.*

SCRANTON, PA.

1885.

ADVERTISEMENT.

Separate Catalogues and Circulars are issued, and will be furnished upon application, containing particulars of

STANDARD GAUGE LOCOMOTIVES,
NARROW GAUGE LOCOMOTIVES,
MINE LOCOMOTIVES FOR OUTSIDE AND INSIDE SERVICE,
LOCOMOTIVES FOR ROLLING MILLS,
CONTRACTORS' LOCOMOTIVES,
PLANTATION LOCOMOTIVES,
LOGGING LOCOMOTIVES,
COMPRESSED AIR LOCOMOTIVES, AND
LOCOMOTIVES FOR ANY SPECIAL SERVICE.

GENERAL MACHINERY.

THE DICKSON MANUFACTURING COMPANY manufacture and issue illustrated catalogues of machinery for the

TRANSMISSION OF POWER,

including, among other things,

SHAFTS of steel, wrought iron, cast iron, and of Phœnix columns, for all purposes and of all sizes.
SHAFT COUPLINGS of all kinds.
SHAFT HANGERS of various kinds.
PEDESTALS of various kinds.
DOUBLE and SINGLE PULLEYS.
ROPE SHEAVES of all kinds and sizes.
FLY WHEELS.
CAST or CUT SPUR and BEVEL WHEELS.
CUT MORTISE SPUR and BEVEL WHEELS.
CAST or CUT WORM WHEELS.
STRAIGHT and CONICAL HOISTING DRUMS for all services.
INCLINED PLANE ROLLERS.
FRICTION CLUTCHES of various kinds.

STATIONARY STEAM ENGINES.

OVER 1,200 OF LARGE SIZES IN SERVICE.

Our steam engines are built at our Penn Avenue and Wilkes-Barre shops, and we have adopted in their construction a system of templets and gauges similar to that used in our locomotive practice, so that duplicates and renewals may be supplied cheaply and economically.

It is our aim to build stationary engines for *long*, *reliable and economical service ;* and we can refer to many which have been running for over twenty years, and are still in use, without having suffered a serious break, or required any considerable repairs.

Our designs are constantly being improved by the suggestions of long experience and the progress of steam-engineering science, worked out by a skilled corps of designers. We use only the very best materials, and employ the most skillful mechanics obtainable, many of whom have been trained in our own shops.

Our facilities for constructing and erecting heavy work in our Penn Avenue shops, which we believe are unsurpassed, and our location in the midst of the anthracite coal region, where fuel costs only a nominal price, enable us to compete on favorable terms for such work.

Our line of steam-engine patterns embraces nearly every kind and size, from the common four-horse power vertical to the heaviest compound.

VERTICAL STEAM ENGINES,

of neat and mechanical design, from 4 H. P. to 75 H. P., with planed and with bored guides. Of heavy and strong proportions for ROLLING MILLS, FACTORIES, etc., up to the largest sizes.

HORIZONTAL STEAM ENGINES.

Box bed and plain or balanced slide valve.

Girder bed   "   "

Trunk bed   "   "

"   with variable cut off.

"   with automatic cut off of superior design.

"   high speed and automatic cut off for electric lighting.

"   with improved Corliss valve gear.

HOISTING ENGINES,

especially designed for contractors' and mine service. These engines are built of great strength for heavy work, usually in pairs, and with either box or girder beds for the smaller sizes from 8″ × 10″ cylinders, to 24″ × 48″ cylinders, the larger sizes of the trunk bed, with bored guides. They are arranged with hoisting drums adapted to the work intended to be done, and provided with all the latest improvements for reversing and control. We have had a long experience in their use at shafts and slopes. The smaller sizes are especially adapted for sinking shafts.

COMPOUND ENGINES.

We build of the "Tandem" or "El Callao" type, of sizes adapted to the work to be done, or with the cylinders in pairs, with a double crank; also with vertical or inclined cylinders of various designs and the most approved valve gear.

PUMPING ENGINES.

Cornish pumping engines and pumps.

Geared pumping engines and pumps.

Water-works pumping engines and pumps of the best designs for high-pressure steam, and HIGH-DUTY COMPOUND ENGINES, of large capacity, from special designs. Our Consulting Engineer, Dr. E. D. Leavitt, Jr., has designed some of the largest and best pumping engines in use.

AIR COMPRESSORS,

to run by steam or other power, of all sizes, for use in mines and for the transmission of power.

BLAST ENGINES,

for Furnaces, Steel Works and Foundries. We have a large variety of patterns for these engines, both horizontal and vertical, single and double. These machines are now doing excellent service in various parts of the country. Blast engines of our make for PNEUMATIC TRANSMISSION, are now in use by the Western Union Telegraph Co. in New York City.

ROLLING-MILL ENGINES,

either double or three cylinder, horizontal or vertical, for reversing trains. Our proximity to the great rail mills has given us considerable experience in the requirements of the modern steel rail mill.

We shall be pleased to submit plans and estimates for special engines of all kinds. A special catalogue of steam engines is now in press.

BOILERS.

Our boiler shops are furnished with the most improved machines for working heavy and large boiler plate, consisting of power bending rolls, plate planers, multiple drills, heavy punches and shears, hydraulic riveters and Tweddell & Platt's hydraulic flanging machine, by means of which we are enabled to flange our boiler heads and flue sheets at one heat without overstraining the metal, and to secure uniformity in size.

We make boilers of all kinds and sizes, using only the best plate, of tested and guaranteed quality.

We have had large experience in designing boilers for the consumption of culm and the waste products of saw mills, factories and tanneries, and are enabled to guarantee a successful and satisfactory result from our designs.

We issue a special catalogue of the products of our boiler shops, which will be furnished on application to those desiring to purchase.

MINING MACHINERY.

Our mechanical engineers have had a long and extensive experience in designing machinery for mining of all kinds, and our stock of plans and patterns is large. Of extra heavy gears and pulleys adapted to the rough work of mines we have an especially large line of patterns.

We offer COAL-BREAKER DESIGNS.

COAL CRACKERS, with patent removable steel teeth and hydraulic extractors. We keep on hand a large stock of finished teeth for renewals, fitted to standards.

PHOSPHATE CRACKERS, fitted to standards.

COAL SCREENS, with Phœnix column shafts and cast-iron shafts.

VENTILATING FANS: the "Guibal," of all sizes.

HOISTING CARRIAGES, with patent safety catch, built very strong, and furnished with boiler-plate canopies, bridle chains and cast-iron landing fans.

BAILING BUCKETS.

HOISTING BUCKETS, with safety hooks.

COAL ELEVATORS.   Chute plates.

MINE CARS, of wood or iron, of various designs.   Car irons.

MINE-CAR WHEELS, FROGS, SWITCHES.

PUMP CHAMBERS and plungers.

COLUMN PIPE.

MINE SKIPS.

STAMP MILLS and AMALGAMATORS.

AIR COMPRESSORS and RECEIVERS.

STEAM and COMPRESSED AIR DRILLS.

ORE-ROASTING OVENS, and all kinds of machinery for MINING, HOISTING and TREATING COAL and ORES.

CONTENTS.

HISTORICAL NOTICE.

EARLY in 1855, the anthracite coal business of the Lackawanna Valley had assumed such proportions that it was deemed necessary that a shop for repairing mining machinery and doing what little new work was needed should be started in the then southern portion of the Lackawanna coal region, and consequently, in February, 1856, Thomas, John A. and George L. Dickson, Maurice and Chas. P. Wurts, Joseph Benjamin and C. T. Pierson came to Scranton from Carbondale, and began the erection of foundry and machine shops, under the name of " Dickson & Co.," and in May of the same year ran the first heat of iron in their foundry, the amount melted being about two tons. They started with about thirty men, the greater number of whom were employed in the foundry. They also had a machine shop and small blacksmith shop. The first few years of the business were not very encouraging, and the complement of men remained about the same, with an average monthly pay roll of about $1,200. A small boiler shop was soon added to the works, but this increased the number of men only by about three, most of the work in that department being repairs for coal works. Notwithstanding the depression of 1857, the works managed to keep in operation, and were enlarged from time to time.

In 1862 the Company was incorporated under the name of "The Dickson Manufacturing Company," with an actual capital of $150,000, and an authorized capital of $300,000. The first officers of the Company were : President, Thomas Dickson ; Secretary and Treasurer, George L. Dickson ; Master Mechanic, John A. Dickson. The number of men employed the first year, i. e., 1862, was about 150, the average daily melting of iron three tons, monthly pay roll about $7,500, and the sales for the first year were $200,000.

As the output of anthracite coal increased, the business of the Company increased with it, and, in 1862, they purchased of Messrs. Cooke & Co. the locomotive shops known as "The Cliff Works," which then had a capacity not exceeding five locomotives per year. In 1864 the "Planing mill" adjoining the Cliff Works was bought, and the manufacture of cars begun. At this time (1865) they employed about 400 men, the daily heats of iron were about four tons, the monthly disbursements to men about $16,000, and the sales over $600,000. In 1866 the foundry and machine shops of Messrs. Lanning & Marshall at Wilkes-Barre were purchased, and a branch established there. At these shops were manufactured car wheels and axles, and such repairs were executed as were needed about the coal works, the number of men employed there at that time being about sixty.

The business of the Company had so increased that in this year the capital was enlarged to $600,000, which, however, was not all issued until 1870.

In 1867 Mr. Thos. Dickson retired from the presidency, and Geo. L. Dickson was elected President in his stead. Mr. Jno. C. Phelps, of Wilkes-Barre, was made Vice-President, and Wm. H. Perkins, Secretary and Treasurer.

With the rapid growth in the valley the Company kept pace, the locomotive shops were enlarged, and in 1869 a large brick foundry was built at the Penn Avenue shops; this helped the business of the Cliff Works as well as the general work, and as additions had, from time to time, been made to the locomotive shops, their capacity was in 1870 four engines per month. The Company then employed about 500 men at their three places, the daily heats of iron aggregated about seven tons, the pay rolls were about $20,000, and the sales amounted to about $975,000. In 1874 the Cliff Works were destroyed by fire, entailing a great loss to the Company. The work of rebuilding was at once begun, and very much improved buildings replaced those burned down, new tools of the most modern design were put in, and the capacity of the shops increased to sixty locomotives per year. In 1876, the capital stock of the Company was further increased to $800,000, at which amount it now stands. In 1878 a large brick building, three stories high, was erected on the corner of Penn Avenue and Vine Street, to be used as a store for the sale of shop and mine supplies, general offices and storage house, and the upper floors for the storage of patterns. The depression of business from 1873 to 1878 was, of course, greatly felt, but all departments were kept at work with a not very large decrease of force. In 1880 about 600 men were employed, with a monthly pay roll of about $30,000, and the sales amounted to about $740,000 per year.

In 1882 Mr. G. L. Dickson resigned from the chair of the presidency and Mr. H. M. Boies was elected. In that year the work of rebuilding the Penn Avenue shops was commenced. A new machine shop was built, which is conceded by experts to be the best arranged shop, for the class of work done, in the country. It covers 223 feet by 100 feet of ground, of which space the machine shop proper occupies 196 feet by 97 feet, together with two galleries 25 feet wide running lengthwise of the building on both sides, giving altogether an available floor space of nearly 29,000 square feet. The remaining part of the ground on the Vine Street end of the building is occupied by a four-story building. In the first story of this building are found, besides the foreman's office in the tower, a large room for the storage of tools and finished work, and also a very well appointed wash room. On the second (or main) floor is the Superintendent's office, a large reading room for the men, and the paymaster's office. On the third floor is the office of the Mechanical Engineer, which has large storage facilities for drawings, the room being fire proof, and adjoining his office is a large, well-appointed draughting office.

A new brick pattern shop was also built, four stories in height (including the basement), 145 feet by 63 feet, the basement being used for storage of lumber, etc., and here also is the power for driving the shop. The first or main floor is used entirely for pattern work, and the upper floors for storage of lumber and patterns.

The Penn Avenue shops were equipped with new tools of the best and most modern design. There was placed in the boiler shop the Tweddell hydraulic system for flanging and riveting. This plant is more fully spoken of in the boiler department of the catalogue.

In 1883 the Company's sales amounted to over $1,400,000, while the average heat of pig iron was twenty-five tons per day.

At present about 1,200 men are employed, with an average monthly pay roll of $50,000.

The capacity of the different shops at the present time is about as follows :

PENN AVENUE SHOPS :—

    600 tons iron melted per month.

    100 stationary engines of all kinds with cylinders over 22 inches in diameter.

    Mining machinery of all kinds.

    Rolling-mill machinery of all kinds.

    Blast-furnace and steel-works machinery.

    Blast engines and air compressors.

    Machine-shop machinery of all kinds.

    Contractors' machinery of all kinds.

    Water-works machinery of all kinds.

    20 boilers per month, including locomotive boilers.

    500 steel plate car wheels per month.

CLIFF WORKS :—

    100 locomotives per year.

WILKES-BARRE SHOPS :—

    150 stationary engines of all kinds with cylinders under 22 inches in diameter.

    Mining machinery of all kinds.

    Wire-rope making machinery of all kinds.

    Cornish pumps of all sizes.

    50 cast-iron plate car wheels per day.

    200 cylinder boilers per year.

PRICES

The prices named herein supersede all previous lists, and are *Subject to Change Without Notice.*

The latest discounts will be given upon application.

TERMS.

All goods will be delivered free on cars or wagons at our works in Wilkes-Barre or Scranton, unless otherwise specified.

Boxing and packing extra, at cost.

Especial attention given to the preparation of machinery for ocean transportation.

Bills will be rendered on delivery, and are required to be paid, unless otherwise agreed, on or before the 20th of the succeeding month.

CIRCULAR OF THE LOCOMOTIVE DEPARTMENT.

GENERAL.

On the following pages we present particulars of locomotives adapted to nearly every variety of service.

Organization and Equipment.—The Locomotive Department of the Dickson Manufacturing Company is entirely separate and distinct in location and organization from the general works, and since its destruction by fire a few years since, has been rebuilt on a more extensive plan, and has been entirely equipped with new machinery from the best machine-tool makers in the country. We thus have the means of doing accurate and well-finished work, and by constant inspection and care of our machinery, excellence in results is secured.

Standards. Interchangeability.—We were among the first to adopt the system of constructing locomotive engines from standard templets and gauges, which we have perfected to such an extent as to guarantee that like parts of locomotives of the same class shall interchange.

Duplicates.—We use a fixed standard of measures and the United States standard screw threads, and can supply duplicate parts with dispatch by reference to the numbers cast or stamped on the various parts. Such a system evidently greatly facilitates repairs, and it enables locomotive users, by keeping a small stock of parts on hand, to reduce the expense of maintenance, and to keep their stock more constantly in service.

Durability.—A considerable experience in repairing locomotives in this vicinity has given us opportunities to discover the parts most likely to require renewing and repairing, and we have given special study in our designs to make these parts durable and easy of access.

METHODS OF MANUFACTURE.

Boilers.—Our Boiler Shop is furnished with the latest and best machinery, and includes a complete hydraulic plant for riveting and flanging the largest sheets.

Efficiency of Hydraulic Machinery.—The hydraulic system of riveting is acknowledged by experts to be the most efficient of the various systems in use, in consequence of the slow movement of the ram, the constancy of the force and the possibility of maintaining the pressure upon the rivet head without diminution until the rivet has set. The slow movement of the ram permits the material of the rivet to flow in a natural way, and experimental joints, which have been riveted by hand, by steam machines and by hydraulic machines, upon being cut through the rivets, invariably show the hydraulic closed rivet to have most perfectly filled the hole, and the plates to have been most perfectly brought together. Plates riveted in this way need less caulking than when riveted by the other systems.

Caulking.—Great care in caulking is taken, at all times, to prevent the under sheet from being injured, and the upper one from being bulged or forced away from the under.

Flanging by Machine.—Flanges turned by our machine are perfectly uniform in appearance, and the material is less likely to be damaged than when turned by hand, as the plate is heated evenly in a special furnace, and the action of the machine is such that the whole flange is turned quickly and simultaneously. This is particularly important with steel plate.

Other Machinery.— Besides the hydraulic machinery above mentioned, the boiler shop is provided with an ample stock of the usual machinery found in first-class boiler works, all of which is of great capacity and power.

Punching.—All punching is done with the Kennedy patent spiral punch, which in reality shears out the material, and thus diminishes, to a great extent, the injury which is known to be caused to the plate in the immediate vicinity of the hole by ordinary punching. The material thus preserves its original elastic limit, and the strength and durability of the joint is considerably increased.

Reaming and Drilling.—We are prepared, however, to undertake, for those who prefer it, to punch the rivet holes small and ream to size, either in place or not, or to drill the holes.

Joints.—We are constantly making boilers with all kinds of joints—simple lap, lap combined with a welt, and butt joints with one or two welts, either single or double riveted.

Steel Plate.—The steel boiler plate used by us is from the best makers, and is guaranteed to have an ultimate tensile strength of 60,000 pounds per square inch, and an elastic limit of 33,000 pounds per square inch.

Tests.—All boilers are subjected to a steam-pressure test before the lagging is put on.

Castings—Forgings.—We make all our own castings from materials best adapting them to the purpose for which they are intended, and forgings from the best refined iron. All hammered iron we make ourselves from No. 1 selected wrought scrap and new bar iron. Connecting rods and frame shapes are forged in one piece, and the jaws of the latter are welded on with a steam drop-hammer, which insures perfect work. All forgings are made in one piece when it is possible.

Brass.—Bearing brasses are made from our own mixtures, which have proved to be satisfactory. In short, it is our aim to use such materials and methods as will make our locomotives strong, durable, economical, and at as low prices as are consistent with these qualities.

Capacity of Works—The capacity of our shops is one hundred and twenty (120) of the ordinary "American" type locomotives per year.

Trials.—We send a competent man to connect and start locomotives.

EXPLANATION OF CLASSIFICATION.

Classification.—In addition to the general remarks on the preceding pages respecting our locomotives, we present the following pages of general specifications of various classes for which we have patterns. The classification is as follows :

CLASS A. 4 coupled wheels locomotive.

" B. 4 coupled wheels locomotive, with a leading 2-wheeled truck.

" C. "American" type of locomotive, having 4 driving wheels and 4 leading truck wheels.

" D. 6 coupled wheels locomotive.

" E. "Mogul" locomotive, having 6 wheels coupled and a 2-wheeled leading truck.

" F. "Ten-Wheel" locomotive, having 6 wheels coupled and a 4-wheeled leading truck.

" G. Locomotive having 8 driving wheels and no truck.

" H. "Consolidation" type of locomotive, having 8 wheels coupled and a 2-wheeled leading truck.

" I. 4 wheels coupled tank switching locomotive, with a 2-wheeled truck behind the driving wheels.

" J. Double-end tank locomotive, with 4 wheels coupled and a 2-wheeled truck at each end.

" K. Tank locomotive of the "Forney" type, having 4 wheels coupled and a trailing 4-wheeled truck under the tank.

" L. Double-end tank locomotive, the same as class K, except with the addition of a leading 2-wheeled truck.

" M. 6 coupled wheels tank switching locomotive, with a trailing 2-wheeled truck.

" N. Same as M, except with the addition of a leading 2-wheeled truck.

" O. 4 coupled wheels "Forney" tank locomotive, with a trailing 4-wheeled truck under the tank.

" P. 6 coupled wheels tank locomotive, with a leading 2-wheeled truck and a trailing 4-wheeled truck, the latter under the tank.

A number prefixed to a class letter indicates the diameter of the cylinder in inches; thus, 18-C means an "American" type locomotive, with cylinders 18 inches in diameter; 20-H means a "Consolidation" type locomotive, with cylinders 20 inches in diameter.

Narrow-Gauge Locomotives.—The above classification refers to locomotives of the 4 feet 8½-inch gauge, and narrower gauges.

Special Classes.—Besides the above-enumerated classes of locomotive, we are prepared to build from special specifications, and from drawings furnished by customers.

Orders.—Orders for locomotives should be accompanied with the following particulars:

1. Gauge of track—exact inside distance between the rails.
2. Limitations of dimensions imposed by tunnels, bridges, etc.
3. Kind and height of car couplings.
4. Kind of fuel to be used.
5. Shipping directions.

Cost of Delivery.—Delivery at any place accessible by rail or water transportation will be included in propositions, if desired.

Other Classes.—We also manufacture locomotives for the following kinds of service, viz.:

MINING, OUTSIDE AND INSIDE USES.

FURNACE.

LOGGING.

PLANTATION.

COMPRESSED-AIR LOCOMOTIVES.

HAULING CAPACITIES.

NOTE.—The hauling capacities of the different locomotives given in the tables which follow, are based upon the assumptions that the resistance of a train is six pounds per ton of weight when moving at five to ten miles per hour, and that the adhesion is equal to one-fifth of the weight on the driving wheels—conditions which are likely to be realized in practice. We have not thought it wise to assume exceptional conditions, but if they should exist, it is obvious that they will be utilized as well as is compatible with the boiler and cylinder capacities, and the weight on the driving wheels. Tables based upon uncommon conditions are only misleading, and with this feeling uppermost, we have considered it inexpedient to publish any letters relating to the work which our locomotives have done, preferring to let every·day facts speak for themselves. We know that our locomotives will haul as heavy loads and keep up their steam as well as any of the same leading dimensions and weights.

The *Grades* given throughout the catalogue are in feet per mile.

Four Wheels Coupled Tank Switching Locomotive.

CLASS A.

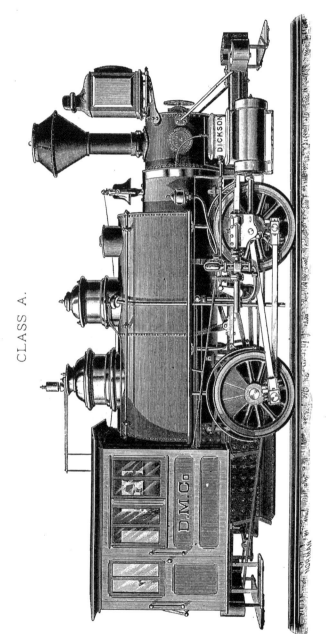

Gauge, 4 Feet 8½ Inches.

FUEL, COAL OR WOOD

Four Wheels Tank Switching Locomotive.

GAUGE, 4 FEET 8½ INCHES, OR WIDER.   FUEL, COAL OR WOOD.

DIMENSIONS AND CAPACITIES OF EIGHT SIZES OF THIS CLASS.

CLASS	9—A	10—A	11—A	12—A	13—A	14—A	15—A	16—A
Cylinders, Diameter	9″	10″	11″	12″	13″	14″	15″	16″
" Stroke	14″ or 16″	16″	16″	18″ to 22″	20″ or 22″	22″	22″	22″ or 24″
Diameter of Driving Wheels	29″ to 36″	30″ to 36″	33″ to 43″	36″ to 45″	36″ to 48″	42″ to 50″	42″ to 50″	42″ to 50″
Wheel Base	5′ 6″	6′ 0″	6′ 0″	7′ 0″	7′ 0″	7′ 0″	7′ 6″	7′ 6″
Length of Engine	19′ 5″	20′ 8″	21′ 7″	24′ 6″	24′ 9″	25′ 2″	26′ 2″	26′ 8″
Weight, Loaded, Total	28,000 lbs.	33,000 lbs.	38,000 lbs.	44,000 lbs.	50,000 lbs.	56,000 lbs.	62,000 lbs.	68,000 lbs.
Capacity of Tank	350 gal.	400 gal.	450 gal.	500 gal.	550 gal.	600 gal.	660 gal.	700 gal.
Hauling Capacity on Level	650 tons.	750 tons.	875 tons.	1,000 tons.	1,150 tons.	1,275 tons.	1,425 tons.	1,550 tons.
" 20 ft. Grade	315	360	420	480	555	615	685	750 "
" 40 ft. "	210	240	280	320	370	410	460	500 "
" 60 ft. "	155	180	210	240	275	305	340	370 "
" 80 ft. "	120	140	165	190	215	240	270	295 "
" 100 ft. "	100	115	135	155	180	200	225	245 "
Prices ready for service at works in Scranton								

Tank Switching Locomotive,

CLASS A.

We present herewith the general dimensions, weights and hauling capacities of a number of the common sizes of the Four-Wheel Tank Switching Engine for the 4' 8½" gauge.   This type of engine is designed specially for switching service in yards and stations, but can be used for short local runs.

The tank is placed on top of the boiler in order to utilize the weight for adhesion, and to dispense with a tender.   By means of this construction the engine is short, and the engine men can observe yard operations somewhat better than if the engine were provided with a tender.   The weight is equally distributed on all driving wheels, and there is a transverse equalizing beam connecting the springs of the forward driving wheels, an arrangement which contributes to steady motion and ease on the rails.

On the next page are given general specifications of this engine as we build them without special instructions.

FRANKLIN IRON CO. No. 1 *Joseph H. Scranton* — Dickson No. 245 - 1879

GENERAL SPECIFICATIONS.

BOILER.—Straight on top, or wagon top with one dome, as may be required. Smoke box made the usual length, using a bonnet or diamond smoke stack, or with an extension and spark arrester inside and a straight smoke stack. Material, best cold-blast charcoal iron, or all-guaranteed steel plate if required; all longitudinal seams on the larger boilers double riveted. Fire box of steel, of ample size for generating steam; flues of best charcoal iron set with copper ferrules in both flue heads; steam dome fitted with balanced throttle valve, one steam whistle and two safety valves of improved make; boiler furnished with steam gauge, blow-off cock, gauge cocks and blower valve, and covered with pine lagging and planished iron jacket; feed water supplied with one pump and one injector, or two injectors as required.

CYLINDERS.—Made of close-grained charcoal iron, as hard as can be worked, outside connected, horizontal, bolted together in center, right and left hand interchangeable, heads, sides and steam chest furnished with iron casings.

PISTONS.—Steel rods, cast-iron heads and followers; packing rings of cast iron or brass.

CROSS HEADS—Of charcoal iron or cast steel.

GUIDE BARS—Of steel, or case-hardened iron, secured to wrought-iron yoke and cylinder head.

CONNECTING RODS.—Best quality hammered iron; boxes of best quality hard brass, lined with babbitt metal.

VALVE MOTION.—Shifting links of hammered iron, with all wearing parts bushed and case hardened; rocker shafts and lifting shafts of wrought iron, with solid arms; cast-iron slide valves of the usual pattern.

DRIVING WHEELS.—Cast-iron centers; steel tires; hammered iron or steel axles as required; axle boxes of cast iron with cast brass bearings; crank pins of steel.

CAB—Of hard wood with plate-glass windows.

TANK.—Mounted on top of boiler.

TOOLS.—A complete set of iron and steel wrenches, one screw wrench, two chisels, hard and soft hammers, two jack screws, one pinch bar, and complete set of fire tools and set of oil cans.

MOUNTING, &c.—Running boards and hand rails on each side; one bell and frame; one or two sand boxes; brackets and shelf for head light; gauge lamp, and all necessary oil cups.

PAINTING.—Engine neatly painted and varnished, and lettered and numbered to suit the purchaser.

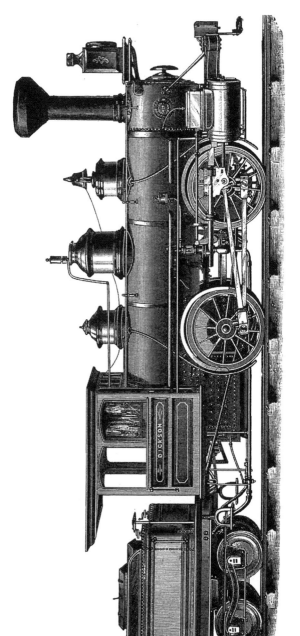

FOUR WHEELS COUPLED SWITCHING LOCOMOTIVE,

WITH TENDER.   CLASS A.

GAUGE, 4 FEET 8½ INCHES.

FUEL, COAL OR WOOD.

Four Wheels Coupled Switching Locomotive—With Tender.

GAUGE, 4 FEET 8½ INCHES.   FUEL, COAL OR WOOD.

DIMENSIONS AND CAPACITIES OF EIGHT SIZES OF THIS CLASS.

CLASS	9–A	10–A	11–A	12–A	13–A	14–A	15–A	16–A
Cylinders, Diameter	9″	10″	11″	12″	13″	14″	15″	16″
" Stroke	14″ or 16″	16″	16″	18″ to 22″	20″ or 22″	22″	22″	22″ or 24″
Diameter of Driving Wheels	29″ to 36″	30″ to 36″	33″ to 48″	36″ to 45″	36″ to 48″	42″ to 50″	42″ to 50″	42″ to 50″
Wheel Base	5′ 6″	6 ft.	6 ft.	7 ft.	7 ft.	7 ft.	7′ 6″	7′ 6″
" " Engine and Tender	28′ 1½″	24′ 7½″	29′ ½″	30′ 6″	31′ 2″	31′ 11″	33′ 1″	33′ 8″
Length of " "	31′ 11″	33′ 8″	38′ 4½″	41′ 3″	42′ 3″	43′ 2″	44′ 6″	45′ 4″
Weight, Loaded, Total	21,000 lbs.	25,000 lbs.	30,000 lbs.	36,000 lbs.	41,000 lbs.	46,000 lbs.	51,000 lbs.	56,000 lbs.
Capacity of Tank	600 gal.	700 gal.	800 gal.	1,000 gal.	1,200 gal.	1,400 gal.	1,600 gal.	1,800 gal.
Hauling Capacity on Level	520 tons.	620 tons.	740 tons.	890 tons.	1,010 tons.	1,180 tons.	1,255 tons.	1,380 tons.
" " 20 ft. Grade	250 "	295 "	355 "	425 "	480 "	540 "	595 "	660 "
" " 40 ft. "	165 "	195 "	235 "	280 "	315 "	355 "	395 "	435 "
" " 60 ft. "	120 "	145 "	170 "	205 "	280 "	260 "	285 "	315 "
" " 80 ft. "	95 "	115 "	135 "	170 "	180 "	205 "	225 "	245 "
" " 100 ft. "	80 "	95 "	110 "	130 "	145 "	165 "	180 "	205 "
Prices ready for service at works in Scranton	$$	$$	$$	$$	$$	$$	$$	$$

Four-Wheel Switching Locomotive.

CLASS A.

WITH TENDER.

We illustrate and give capacities of our Four-Wheel Switching Locomotive, with Tender, on the two preceding pages. It is designed for switching service in yards or stations, and can also be used for short runs on local roads.

The weight of the engine is equally distributed among the four driving wheels, and the front ends of the forward springs are connected by a transverse equalizing lever, which contributes to steadiness of motion and ease upon the road bed.

The tender is built with six wheels or two four-wheel trucks.

General specifications are given on the next page.

HOUSTON & TEXAS CENTRAL RY. No. 70 *Bison* – Dickson No. 197 – 1876

GENERAL SPECIFICATIONS.

BOILER.—Straight on top, or wagon top with one dome, as may be required. Smoke box made the usual length, using a bonnet or diamond smoke stack, or with an extension and spark arrester inside and a straight smoke stack. Material, best cold-blast charcoal iron, or all-guaranteed steel plate if required; all longitudinal seams on the larger boilers double riveted. Fire box of steel, of ample size for generating steam; flues of best charcoal iron set with copper ferrules in both flue heads; steam dome fitted with balanced throttle valve, one steam whistle and two safety valves of improved make; boiler furnished with steam gauge, blow-off cock, gauge cocks and blower valve, and covered with pine lagging and planished iron jacket; feed water supplied with one pump and one injector, or two injectors, as required.

CYLINDERS.—Made of close-grained charcoal iron, as hard as can be worked, outside connected, horizontal, bolted together in center, right and left hand interchangeable, heads, sides and steam chest furnished with iron casings.

PISTONS.—Steel rods, cast-iron heads and followers; packing rings of cast iron or brass.

CROSS HEADS—Of charcoal iron or cast steel.

GUIDE BARS—Of steel, secured to wrought iron yoke and cylinder head.

CONNECTING RODS.—Best quality hammered iron; boxes of best quality hard brass, lined with babbitt metal.

VALVE MOTION.—Shifting links of hammered iron, with all wearing parts bushed and case hardened; rocker shafts and lifting shaft of wrought iron, with solid arms; cast-iron slide valves of the usual pattern.

DRIVING WHEELS.—Cast-iron centers; steel tires; hammered iron or steel axles if required; axle boxes of cast iron with cast brass bearings; crank pins of steel.

CAB—Of hard wood with plate-glass windows.

TANK—Of ample capacity, made straight on top with flanges on sides and back, or made sloping on back to give the engineer a clear view in the rear. Mounted on either an oak or an iron frame, with four or six wheels, or two four-wheel trucks; wheels double plate, chilled face, hammered iron axles with brass bearings.

TOOLS.—A complete set of iron and steel wrenches, one screw wrench, two chisels, hard and soft hammers, two jack screws, one pinch bar, and complete set of fire tools and set of oil cans.

MOUNTING, &c.—Running boards and hand rails on each side; one bell and frame; one or two sand boxes; brackets and shelf for head light; gauge lamp, and all necessary oil cups.

PAINTING.—Engine and tender neatly painted and varnished, and lettered and numbered to suit the purchaser.

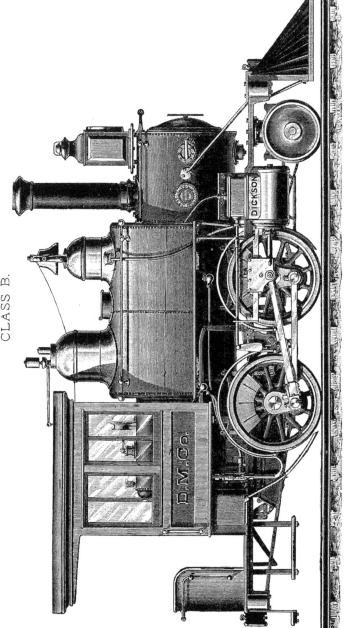

TANK SWITCHING ENGINE.

CLASS B.

GAUGE, 4 FEET 8½ INCHES.

FUEL, COAL OR WOOD.

TANK SWITCHING ENGINE.

GAUGE, 4 FEET 8½ INCHES. FUEL, COAL OR WOOD.

DIMENSIONS AND CAPACITIES OF EIGHT SIZES OF THIS CLASS.

CLASS.	10—B	11—B	12—B	13—B	14—B	15—B	16—B	17—B
Cylinders, Diameter	10″	11″	12″	13″	14″	15″	16″	17″
" Stroke	16″	16″	18″	20″	22″	22″	22″ or 24″	22″ or 24″
Diameter of Driving Wheels	33″ to 40″	36″ to 42″	36″ to 45″	36″ to 48″	40″ to 50″	42″ to 54″	42″ to 54″	44″ to 56″
" Truck Wheels	22″ to 24″	24″ to 26″	24″ to 26″	24″ to 28″	26″ to 30″	26″ to 30″	26″ to 30″	28″ to 30″
Wheel Base, Rigid	5′ 3″	5′ 6″	5′ 9″	6′ 0″	6′ 6″	7′ 0″	7′ 6″	7′ 6″
" Total	11′ 1″	11′ 6″	12′ 2″	12′ 10″	13′ 7″	14′ 3″	15′ 0″	15′ 6″
Length of Engine without Pilot	20′ 10″	21′ 10″	23′ 0″	24′ 3″	25′ 3″	26′ 3″	27′ 6″	28′ 6″
" with one Pilot	23′ 6″	24′ 9″	26′ 0″	27′ 3″	28′ 3″	29′ 6″	30′ 9″	31′ 9″
Weight, Loaded, Total	34,000 lbs.	40,000 lbs.	46,000 lbs.	52,000 lbs.	58,000 lbs.	64,000 lbs.	70,000 lbs.	76,000 lbs.
" on Drivers	26,000 "	31,000 "	36,000 "	42,000 "	47,000 "	53,000 "	58,000 "	64,000 "
" on Trucks	8,000 "	9,000 "	10,000 "	10,000 "	11,000 "	11,000 "	12,000 "	12,000 "
Capacity of Tank	400 gal.	450 gal.	500 gal.	550 gal.	600 gal.	700 gal.	800 gal.	900 ga.
Hauling Capacity on Level	600 tons.	725 tons.	850 tons.	975 tons.	1,100 tons.	1,250 tons.	1,400 tons.	1,550 tons.
" " 20 ft. Grade	290 "	350 "	410 "	460 "	530 "	605 "	680 "	750 "
" " 40 ft. "	195 "	235 "	275 "	315 "	355 "	405 "	455 "	500 "
" " 60 ft. "	145 "	175 "	205 "	235 "	265 "	300 "	335 "	370 "
" " 80 ft. "	115 "	140 "	160 "	185 "	210 "	240 "	265 "	295 "
" " 100 ft. "	95 "	115 "	135 "	155 "	175 "	200 "	220 "	245 "
Prices ready for service at works in Scranton	$	$	$	$	$	$	$	$

Tank Switching Locomotive.

CLASS B.

The Class " B " Tank Switching Locomotive, of which we present the leading particulars of various sizes, is designed chiefly for switching purposes, but can be used to draw suburban service trains with satisfaction on account of the leading swing-bolster, radius-bar truck. This keeps the engine steady at the higher speeds, and allows it to take curves with ease.

General specifications are given on the following page.

GENERAL SPECIFICATIONS.

BOILER.—Made of best cold-blast charcoal plate iron, or all-guaranteed steel plate if required; longitudinal seams double riveted for the larger sizes. Fire box of steel, tubes of best wrought iron set with copper ferrules at both ends; one steam dome fitted with balanced throttle valve; one steam whistle and two safety valves; feed water supplied with one pump and one injector (or two injectors if required); boiler furnished with steam gauge, blow-off cock, gauge cocks and blower valve, and covered with pine lagging and planished iron jacket.

CYLINDERS.—Made of close-grained charcoal iron, as hard as can be worked, outside connected, horizontal, bolted together in center, right and left hand interchangeable. heads, sides and steam chest furnished with iron casings.

PISTONS.—Steel rods, cast-iron heads and followers; packing rings of cast iron or brass.

CROSS HEADS—Of charcoal iron or cast steel.

GUIDE BARS—Of steel, or case-hardened iron, secured to wrought-iron yoke and cylinder head.

CONNECTING RODS.—Best quality hammered iron; boxes of best quality hard brass, lined with babbitt metal.

VALVE MOTION.—Shifting links of hammered iron, case hardened, with all wearing parts bushed and case hardened; rocker shafts and lifting shaft of wrought iron, with solid arms; cast-iron slide valves of the usual pattern.

DRIVING WHEELS.—Cast-iron centers; steel tires; hammered iron or steel axles, if required; axle boxes of cast iron with brass bearings; crank pins of steel.

TRUCK.—Swing bolster, with radius bar; chilled wheels; hammered iron axle; cast-iron axle boxes with brass bearings.

CAB—Of hard wood with plate-glass windows.

PILOT—Of hard wood or wrought iron.

TANK.—Mounted on top of boiler.

TOOLS.—A complete set of iron and steel wrenches. one screw wrench, two chisels, hard and soft hammers, two jack screws, one pinch bar, and complete set of fire tools.

MOUNTING, &c.—Running boards and hand rails on each side; one bell and frame; one sand box; brackets and shelf for head light; signal gong; steam gauge lamp, and all necessary oil cans and oil cups.

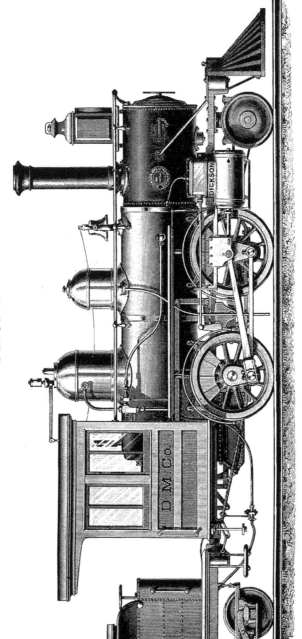

PASSENGER OR SWITCHING ENGINE—WITH TENDER.

CLASS B.

GAUGE, 4 FEET 8½ INCHES.

FUEL, COAL OR WOOD.

PASSENGER OR SWITCHING ENGINE—WITH TENDER.

GAUGE, 4 FEET 8½ INCHES.   FUEL, COAL OR WOOD.

DIMENSIONS AND CAPACITIES OF EIGHT SIZES OF THIS CLASS.

CLASS.	10—B	11—B	12—B	13—B	14—B	15—B	16—B	17—B
Cylinders, Diameter	10″	11″	12″	13″	14″	15″	16″	17″
" Stroke	16″	16″	18″	20″	22″	22″	22″ or 24″	22″ or 24″
Diameter of Driving Wheels	33″ to 40″	36″ to 42″	36″ to 45″	36″ to 48″	40″ to 50″	42″ to 54″	42″ to 54″	44″ to 56″
" Truck Wheels	22″ to 24″	24″ to 26″	24″ to 26″	24″ to 28″	26″ to 30″	26″ to 30″	26″ to 30″	28″ to 30″
Wheel Base, Rigid	5′ 3″	5′ 6″	5′ 9″	6′ 0″	6′ 6″	7′ 0″	7′ 6″	7′ 6″
" " Total	11′ 1″	11′ 6″	12′ 2″	12′ 10″	13′ 7″	14′ 3″	15′ 0″	15′ 6″
" " Engine and Tender	27′ 0″	31′ 9″	32′ 0″	34′ 4″	35′ 10″	37′ 1″	38′ 6″	39′ 6″
Length of Engine and Tender, one Pilot	35′ 0″	39′ 10″	41′ 0″	43′ 3″	44′ 9″	46′ 4″.	47′ 9″	48′ 9″
Weight, Loaded, Total	28,000 lbs.	33,000 lbs.	38,000 lbs.	43,000 lbs.	48,000 lbs.	53,000 lbs.	58,000 lbs.	63,000 lbs.
" on Drivers	21,000 "	26,000 "	30,000 "	35,000 "	40,000 "	45,000 "	49,000 "	54,000 "
" on Trucks	7,000 "	7,000 "	8,000 "	8,000 "	8,000 "	8,000 "	9,000 "	9,000 "
Capacity of Tank	900 gal.	1,000 gal.	1,100 gal.	1,200 gal.	1,400 gal.	1,600 gal.	1,800 gal.	2,000 gal.
Hauling Capacity on Level	515 tons.	640 tons.	735 tons.	860 tons.	985 tons.	1,105 tons.	1,205 tons.	1,330 tons.
" " 20 ft. Grade	245 "	305 "	350 "	410 "	470 "	525 "	575 "	635 "
" " 40 ft. "	160 "	200 "	230 "	270 "	310 "	345 "	375 "	415 "
" " 60 ft. "	115 "	145 "	165 "	195 "	225 "	250 "	275 "	305 "
" " 80 ft. "	90 "	115 "	130 "	150 "	175 "	195 "	215 "	235 "
" " 100 ft. "	75 "	95 "	105 "	125 "	145 "	160 "	175 "	195 "
Prices ready for service at works in Scranton	$	$	$	$	$	$	$	$

Passenger or Switching Engine.

CLASS B.

The Class " B " Passenger or Switching Engine, of which particulars are here-with given, is designed for the passenger or general service of suburban or branch roads, or for switching service. The leading truck, which has a swing bolster and radius bar, keeps the engine steady at the higher speeds, and allows it to take curves with ease.

General specifications are given on the next page.

GENERAL SPECIFICATIONS.

BOILER.—Made of best cold-blast charcoal plate iron, or all-guaranteed steel plate if required; longitudinal seams double riveted for the larger sizes.   Fire box of steel, tubes of best wrought iron set with copper ferrules at both ends; one steam dome fitted with balanced throttle valve; one steam whistle and two safety valves; feed water supplied with one pump and one injector (or two injectors if required); boiler furnished with steam gauge, blow-off cock, gauge cocks and blower valve, and covered with pine lagging and planished iron jacket.

CYLINDERS.—Made of close-grained charcoal iron, as hard as can be worked, outside connected, horizontal, bolted together in center, right and left hand interchangeable, heads, sides and steam chest furnished with iron casings.

PISTONS.—Steel rods, cast-iron heads and followers; packing rings of cast iron or brass.

CROSS HEADS—Of charcoal iron or cast steel.

GUIDE BARS—Of steel, or case-hardened iron, secured to wrought-iron yoke and cylinder head.

CONNECTING RODS.—Best quality hammered iron; boxes of best quality hard brass, lined with babbitt metal.

VALVE MOTION.—Shifting links of hammered iron, case hardened, with all wearing parts bushed and case hardened; rocker shafts and lifting shaft of wrought iron, with solid arms; cast-iron slide valves of the usual pattern.

DRIVING WHEELS.—Cast-iron centers; steel tires; hammered iron or steel axles, if required; axle boxes of cast iron with brass bearings; crank pins of steel.

ENGINE TRUCK.—Swing bolster, with radius bar; chilled wheels; hammered iron axles; cast-iron axle boxes with brass bearings.

CAB—Of hard wood with plate-glass windows.

PILOT—Of hard wood or wrought iron.

TANK.—Mounted on oak or iron frame, with four wheels or two four-wheeled trucks; wheels double plate, chilled face; hammered iron axles with brass bearings.

TOOLS.—A complete set of iron and steel wrenches, one screw wrench, two chisels, hard and soft hammers, two jack screws, one pinch bar, and complete set of fire tools.

MOUNTING, &c.—Running boards and hand rails on each side; one bell and frame; one sand box; brackets and shelf for head light; signal gong; steam gauge lamp, and all necessary oil cans and oil cups.

"AMERICAN" TYPE LOCOMOTIVE—FOR PASSENGER OR FREIGHT SERVICE.

CLASS C.

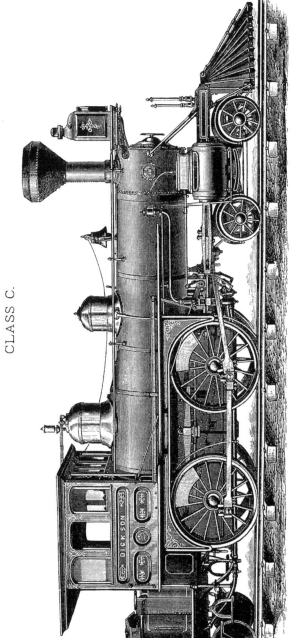

GAUGE, 4 FEET 8½ INCHES.

FUEL, ANTHRACITE COAL.

"AMERICAN" TYPE LOCOMOTIVE—FOR PASSENGER OR FREIGHT SERVICE.

GAUGE, 4 FEET 8½ INCHES. FUEL, ANTHRACITE COAL.

DIMENSIONS AND CAPACITIES OF NINE SIZES OF THIS CLASS.

CLASS.	12-C	13-C	14-C	15-C	16-C	17-C	18-C	19-C	20-C
Cylinders, Diameter	12"	13"	14"	15"	16"	17"	18"	19"	20"
" Stroke	20" to 22"	20" to 22"	22" to 24"	22" to 24"	22" to 24"	22" to 24"	22" to 24"	22" to 24"	22" to 24"
Diameter of Driving Wheels	44" to 56"	48" to 60"	48" to 62"	56" to 60"	56" to 68"	56" to 68"	56" to 68"	56" to 68"	56" to 72"
" Truck Wheels	24" to 26"	24" to 28"	26" to 28"	26" to 28"	26" to 30"	26" to 30"	26" to 30"	26" to 30"	26" to 30"
Wheel Base, Rigid	6' 6"	7' 0"	7' 3"	7' 6"	7' 6"	8' 0"	8' 3"	8' 6"	8' 9"
" " Total	19' 6"	20' 4"	20' 10"	21' 2"	21' 2"	21' 11"	22' 3"	22' 8"	22' 11"
" " Engine and Tender	40' 4"	41' 2"	41' 8"	41' 3"	42' 3"	44' 2"	45' 0"	46' 6"	47' 6"
Length of Engine and Tender	48' 11"	49' 9"	50' 11"	49' 8"	50' 8"	53' 10"	54' 8"	56' 1"	57' 3"
Weight, Loaded, Total	48,000 lbs.	53,000 lbs.	58,000 lbs.	64,000 lbs.	70,000 lbs.	76,000 lbs.	83,000 lbs.	90,000 lbs.	98,000 lbs.
" on Drivers	32,000	35,000	39,000	44,000	48,000	53,000	60,000	66,000	73,000
" on Trucks	16,000	18,000	19,000	20,000	22,000	23,000	23,000	24,000	25,000
Capacity of Tank	1,400 gal.	1,500 gal.	1,800 gal.	2,000 gal.	2,000 gal.	2,400 gal.	2,600 gal.	2,800 gal.	3,000 gal.
Hauling Capacity on Level	785 tons.	855 tons.	955 tons.	1,075 tons.	1,175 tons.	1,300 tons.	1,470 tons.	1,620 tons.	1,800 tons.
" 20 ft. Grade	370	405	450	505	555	615	695	770	855
" 40 ft. "	235	265	295	380	365	405	455	505	560
" 60 ft. "	175	190	215	240	265	295	380	365	410
" 80 ft. "	135	145	165	185	205	230	255	285	320
" 100 ft. "	110	120	135	150	165	185	205	230	260
Prices ready for service at works in Scranton	$	$	$	$	$	$	$	$	$

"American" Type Locomotive.

Class C.

FUEL, ANTHRACITE COAL.

We devote the two preceding pages to representations and particulars of what has been of late years called, by general consent, the "American" type of locomotive, as we build them for burning anthracite coal. It has received the name, not because engines nearly identical in design with it have not been used in other countries, but because it is extremely popular and common in the United States, and is regarded here as the most fit type for conducting nearly all passenger service, and all freight service within the limits of its capacity. As offered by the best builders it is probably the cheapest machine for its weight and power made, and there is but little opportunity for distinguishing characteristics as designed by different manufacturers.

The forward end of the locomotive rests on a pivot on the truck which permits the truck to turn and accommodate itself to curvature of track, and on crooked or poorly aligned roads the pivot is permitted to have some lateral movement by means of the " swing bolster " of the truck. The rear end of the engine rests on the driving wheels, through the intervention of equalizing levers or beams, the effect of which arrangement, it can be shown, is that each side of the back end of the locomotive rests on a single point. This property, taken in connection with the central support at the truck, is very important, as it is equivalent to the whole loco-motive resting on three points, an arrangement which is in accordance with the mechanical principle that when a body rests on three points it is absolutely free to accommodate itself to them. It should also be stated that an effect of equalizing beams is to give the wheels great vertical flexibility in their movements when passing over inequalities of the track.

In the larger sizes of this locomotive the fire box is placed entirely above the frame, in order to gain grate surface. When this is done, the frame slants down as it goes from the back to the forward axle, and joins the jaw opposite the axle center. This enables the proper depth of fire box to be secured forward.

To the features of the design of this type of locomotive, as briefly described above, are to be ascribed its success in this country, as it will run steadily and keep on tracks so poorly constructed as to cause a less flexible engine to leave the rails.

Below we present general specifications of this type of engine as we build them in the absence of special directions.

GENERAL SPECIFICATIONS.

BOILER.—Made of best cold-blast charcoal plate iron, or all-guaranteed steel plate if required; longitudinal seams double riveted. Fire box of steel, tubes of best wrought iron set with copper ferrules at both ends; one steam dome fitted with balanced throttle valve; one steam whistle and two safety valves; feed water supplied with one pump and one injector (or two injectors if required); boiler furnished with steam gauge, blow-off cock, gauge cocks and blower valve, and covered with pine lagging and planished iron jacket.

CYLINDERS.—Made of close-grained charcoal iron, as hard as can be worked, outside connected, horizontal, bolted together in center, right and left hand interchangeable, heads, sides and steam chest furnished with iron casings.

PISTONS.—Steel rods, cast-iron heads and followers; packing rings of cast iron or brass.

CROSS HEADS—Of charcoal iron or cast steel.

GUIDE BARS—Of steel, or case-hardened iron, secured to wrought-iron yoke and cylinder head.

CONNECTING RODS.—Best quality hammered iron; boxes of best quality hard brass, lined with babbitt metal.

VALVE MOTION.—Shifting links of hammered iron, case hardened, with all wearing parts bushed and case hardened; rocker shafts and lifting shaft of wrought iron, with solid arms; cast-iron slide valves of the usual pattern.

DRIVING WHEELS.—Cast-iron centers; steel tires; hammered iron or steel axles as required; axle boxes of cast iron with brass bearings; crank pins of steel.

ENGINE TRUCK.—Swing bolster, with radius bar; chilled wheels; hammered iron axles; cast-iron axle boxes with brass bearings.

CAB—Of hard wood with plate-glass windows.

PILOT—Of hard wood or wrought iron.

TANK.—Mounted on either an oak or an iron frame, with two four-wheeled trucks; wheels double plate, chilled face; hammered iron axles with brass bearings.

TOOLS.—A complete set of iron and steel wrenches, one screw wrench, two chisels, hard and soft hammers, two jack screws, one pinch bar, and complete set of fire tools.

MOUNTING, &c.—Running boards and hand rails on each side; one bell and frame; one sand box; brackets and shelf for head light; signal gong; steam gauge lamp, and all necessary oil cans and oil cups.

"AMERICAN" TYPE LOCOMOTIVE—FOR PASSENGER OR FREIGHT SERVICE.

CLASS C.

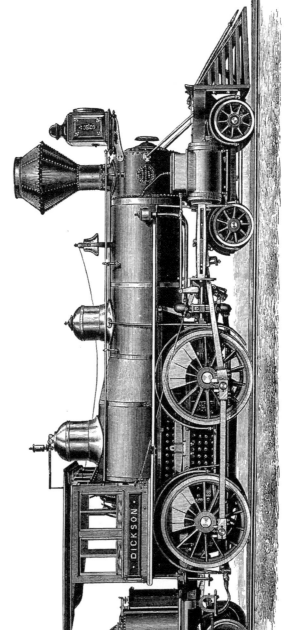

GAUGE, 4 FEET 8½ INCHES.

FUEL, BITUMINOUS COAL, OR WOOD.

"AMERICAN" TYPE LOCOMOTIVE.

FUEL, BITUMINOUS COAL, OR WOOD.
GAUGE, 4 FEET 8½ INCHES.

DIMENSIONS AND CAPACITIES OF TEN SIZES OF THIS CLASS.

CLASS	10-C	11-C	12-C	13-C	14-C	15-C	16-C	17-C	18-C	19-C
Cylinders, Diameter	10″	11″	12″	13″	14″	15″	16″	17″	18″	19″
" Stroke	18″ to 20″	18″ to 20″	20″ to 22″	20″ to 22″	22″ to 24″	22″ to 24″	22″ to 24″	22″ to 24″	22″ to 24″	22″ to 24″
Diameter of Driving Wheels	44″ to 56″	44″ to 56″	44″ to 56″	48″ to 60″	48″ to 62″	56″ to 66″	56″ to 68″	56″ to 68″	56″ to 68″	56″ to 68″
" Truck Wheels	24″ to 26″	24″ to 26″	24″ to 26″	24″ to 28″	26″ to 28″	26″ to 28″	26″ to 30″	26″ to 30″	26″ to 30″	26″ to 30″
Wheel Base Rigid	5′–6″	6′ ft.	6′–6″	7′ ft.	7′–3″	7′–6″	8′ ft.	8′–3″	8′–6″	8′–9″
" Total	17′–3″	18′–9″	19′–6″	20′–4″	20′–10″	21′–2″	21′–8″	22′–2″	22′–5″	22′–11″
" " Engine and Tender	36′–3″	37′–11″	38′–8″	39′–8″	40′–5″	40′–9″	41′–3″	41′–9″	43′ ft.	48′–7″
Length of Engine and Tender	44′–6″	46′–2″	46′–11″	48′–3″	48′–8″	49′–2″	49′–8″	51′–5″	53′ ft.	53′–7″
Weight Loaded, Total	37,000 lbs.	42,000 lbs.	46,000 lbs.	50,000 lbs.	55,000 lbs.	60,000 lbs.	65,000 lbs.	72,000 lbs.	79,000 lbs.	86,000 lbs.
" on Drivers	24,000 lbs.	28,000 lbs.	30,000 lbs.	33,000 lbs.	37,000 lbs.	40,000 lbs.	43,000 lbs.	48,000 lbs.	53,000 lbs.	58,000 lbs.
" " Trucks	13,000 lbs.	14,000 lbs.	16,000 lbs.	17,000 lbs.	18,000 lbs.	20,000 lbs.	22,000 lbs.	24,000 lbs.	26,000 lbs.	28,000 lbs.
Capacity of Tank	1,000 gal.	1,100 gal.	1,400 gal.	1,500 gal.	2,000 gal.	2,000 gal.	2,200 gal.	2,400 gal.	2,600 gal.	2,800 gal.
Hauling Capacity on Level	585 tons.	685 tons.	735 tons.	805 tons.	905 tons.	975 tons.	1,050 tons.	1,175 tons.	1,295 tons.	1,420 tons.
" 20 ft. Grade	275 "	325 "	350 "	380 "	430 "	460 "	495 "	555 "	610 "	770 "
" 40 ft. "	180 "	210 "	230 "	250 "	280 "	300 "	325 "	365 "	400 "	440 "
" 60 ft. "	130 "	155 "	165 "	180 "	206 "	215 "	235 "	265 "	290 "	320 "
" 80 ft. "	100 "	120 "	130 "	140 "	155 "	165 "	180 "	205 "	225 "	245 "
" 100 ft. "	80 "	95 "	105 "	110 "	125 "	135 "	145 "	165 "	180 "	200 "
Price ready for service at Works in Scranton										

"AMERICAN" TYPE LOCOMOTIVE.

CLASS C.

FUEL, BITUMINOUS COAL OR WOOD.

On the two preceding pages we present an engraving and particulars of the "American" type of locomotive, as built by us for burning bituminous coal or wood.

The design differs from the preceding only in those respects which are due to the nature of the fuel for which it is intended, and the general remarks on page 38 apply equally well to the present case.

The fire box of this locomotive is between the driving-wheel axles, and necessitates, for the larger sizes of engines, a greater spread of wheels than in the other, as in the latter case the fire box is above the rear axle.

The general specifications are given on page 39.

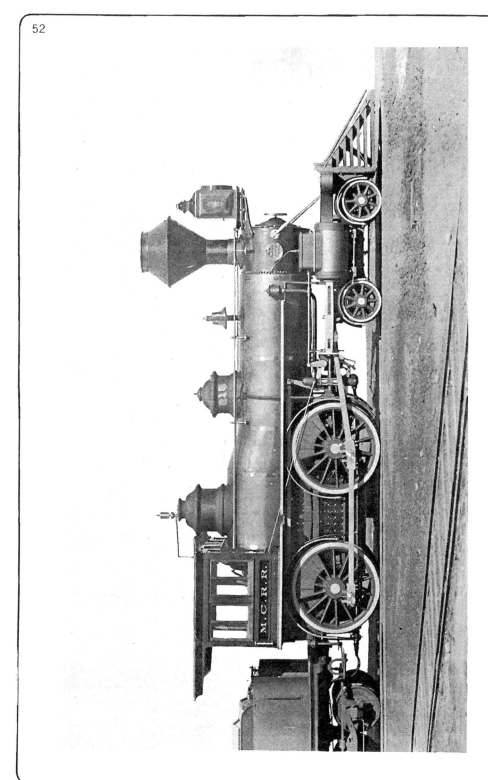

MICHIGAN CENTRAL RR No. 218 — Dickson No. 214 — 1879

SIX WHEELS COUPLED TANK SWITCHING LOCOMOTIVE.

CLASS D.

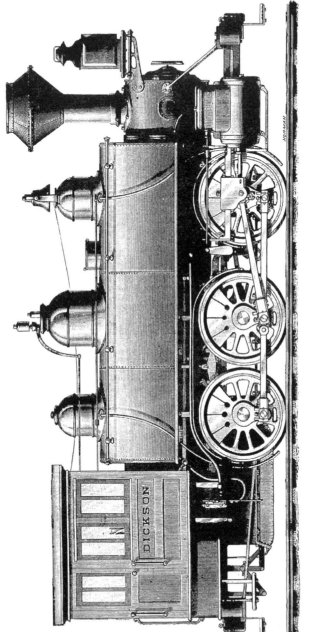

GAUGE, 4 FEET 8½ INCHES.

FUEL, COAL OR WOOD.

SIX WHEELS COUPLED TANK SWITCHING LOCOMOTIVE.

CLASS D.

GAUGE, 4 FEET 8½ INCHES.

FUEL, COAL OR WOOD.

SIX WHEELS COUPLED TANK SWITCHING LOCOMOTIVE.

GAUGE, 4 FEET 8½ INCHES.   FUEL, COAL OR WOOD.

DIMENSIONS AND CAPACITIES OF SIX SIZES OF THIS CLASS.

CLASS.	14—D	15—D	16—D	17—D	18—D	19—D
Cylinders, Diameter	14″	15″	16″	17″	18′	19′
" Stroke	22″	22″	22″ or 24″	22″ or 24″	22″ or 24″	22″ or 24″
Diameter of Driving Wheels	42′ to 50′	42′ to 50″	42″ to 50″	42″ to 50″	42″ to 50″	42″ to 50″
Wheel Base, Rigid	9′ 0′	10 ft.	10 ft.	10′ 3″	10′ 6″	10′ 9″
Length of Engine	27′ 7′	28′ 1½″	28′ 9″	29′ 5′	30′ 1′	30′ 8′
Weight Loaded, Total	67,000 lbs.	78,000 lbs.	79,000 lbs.	85,000 lbs.	91,000 lbs.	97,000 lbs.
Capacity of Tank	700 gal.	750 gal.	850 gal.	900 gal.	950 gal.	1,000 gal.
Hauling Capacity on Level	1,600 tons.	1,750 tons.	1,900 tons.	2,025 tons.	2,175 tons.	2,325 tons.
" " 20 ft. Grade	775 "	850 "	920 "	980 "	1,055 "	1,125 "
" " 40 ft. "	530 "	570 "	615 "	655 "	705 "	755 "
" " 60 ft. "	365 "	420 "	455 "	485 "	525 "	560 "
" " 80 ft. "	305 "	235 "	365 "	385 "	415 "	445 "
" " 100 ft. "	255 "	280 "	300 "	320 "	345 "	370 "
Price ready for service at works in Scranton	$	$	$	$	$	$

Six-Wheel Tank Switching Engine.

CLASS D.

We devote the three preceding pages to views and particulars of the Six-Wheel Tank Switching Engine, which is designed for switching service in yards and depots of stations, and can also be used for short runs on local roads.

These engines are built with the tank placed either on the top or sides of the boiler, thereby utilizing all the weight for adhesion, which is equally distributed among the wheels. There is an equalizing lever between the middle and back driving wheels on each side, and the front driving wheels are equalized transversely, thus giving the engine an easy and steady motion.

General specifications will be found on the following page.

DELAWARE & HUDSON CANAL CO. No. 163 *Ajax* – Dickson No. 267 – 1880

GENERAL SPECIFICATIONS.

BOILER.—Straight on top, or wagon top, as may be required. Smoke box made the usual length, using a bonnet or diamond smoke stack, or with an extension and spark arrester inside and a straight smoke stack. Material, best cold-blast charcoal iron, or all-guaranteed steel plate if required; all longitudinal seams on the larger boilers double riveted. Fire box of steel, of ample size for generating steam; tubes of best charcoal iron set with copper ferrules in both tube sheets; steam dome fitted with balanced throttle valve, one steam whistle and two safety valves of improved make; boiler furnished with steam gauge, blow-off cock, gauge cocks and blower valve, and covered with pine lagging and planished iron jacket; feed water supplied with one pump and one injector, or two injectors as required.

CYLINDERS.—Made of close-grained charcoal iron, as hard as can be worked, outside connected, horizontal, bolted together in center, right and left hand interchangeable, heads, sides and steam chest furnished with iron casings.

PISTONS.—Steel rods, cast-iron heads and followers; packing rings of cast iron or brass.

CROSS HEADS—Of charcoal iron or cast steel.

GUIDE BARS—Of steel, or case-hardened iron, secured to wrought-iron yoke and cylinder head.

CONNECTING RODS.—Best quality hammered iron; boxes of best quality hard brass, lined with babbitt metal.

VALVE MOTION.—Shifting links of hammered iron, with all wearing parts bushed and case hardened; rocker shafts and lifting shafts of wrought iron, with solid arms; cast-iron slide valves of the usual pattern.

DRIVING WHEELS.—Cast-iron centers; steel tires; hammered iron or steel axles as required; axle boxes of cast iron with cast brass bearings; crank pins of steel. Unless otherwise ordered on this class of locomotive we put flanges on all the wheels, but can make the middle pair of wheels with plain tires if required.

CAB—Of hard wood with plate-glass windows.

TANK.—Mounted either on top or sides of boiler.

TOOLS.—A complete set of iron and steel wrenches, one screw wrench, two chisels, hard and soft hammers, two jack screws, one pinch bar, and complete set of fire tools and set of oil cans.

MOUNTING, &c.—Running boards and hand rails on each side; one bell and frame; one or two sand boxes; brackets and shelf for head light; gauge lamp, and all necessary oil cups.

PAINTING.—Engine and tender neatly painted and varnished, and lettered and numbered to suit the purchaser.

Six Wheels Coupled Switching Locomotive.

With Tender.   Class D.

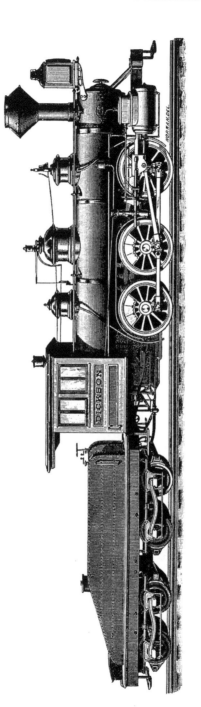

Gauge, 4 Feet 8½ Inches.

Fuel, Coal or Wood.

DETROIT, SAGINAW & BAY CITY RR No. 15 – Dickson No. 263 – 1880

Six Wheels Switching Engine—With Tender.

GAUGE, 4 FEET 8½ INCHES.   FUEL, COAL OR WOOD.

DIMENSIONS AND CAPACITIES OF SIX SIZES OF THIS CLASS.

CLASS	14–D	15–D	16–D	17–D	18–D	19–D
Cylinders, Diameter	14″	15″	16″	17″	18″	19″
" Stroke	22″	22″	22″ or 24″	22″ or 24″	22″ or 24″	22″ or 24″
Diameter of Driving Wheels	42″ to 50″	42″ to 50″	42″ to 50″	42″ to 50″	42″ to 50″	42″ to 50″
Wheel Base, Rigid	9′ 9″	10 ft.	10 ft.	10′ 3″	10 6″	10′ 9″
" " Engine and Tender	37′ 9″	38′ 1½″	39′ 1½″	39′ 9″	40′ 7″	41′ 2″
Length of " " "	45′ 3″	46′ 1½″	46′ 7½″	47′ 3″	48′ 1″	48′ 8″
Weight Loaded, Total	55,000 lbs.	60,000 lbs.	65,000 lbs.	70,000 lbs.	75,000 lbs.	80,000 lbs.
Capacity of Tank	1,500 gal.	1,600 gal.	1,800 gal.	2,000 gal.	2,200 gal.	2,400 gal.
Hauling Capacity on Level	1,360 tons.	1,480 tons.	1,605 tons.	1,780 tons.	1,850 tons.	1,975 tons.
" 20 ft. Grade	650 "	705 "	765 "	820 "	885 "	945 "
" 40 ft. "	430 "	465 "	505 "	550 "	605 "	625 "
" 60 ft. "	315 "	340 "	370 "	400 "	425 "	455 "
" 80 ft. "	250 "	265 "	290 "	315 "	335 "	360 "
" 100 ft. "	205 "	220 "	240 "	280 "	275 "	295 "
Price ready for service at works in Scranton	$	$	$	$	$	$

Six-Wheel Switching Locomotive.

CLASS D.

WITH TENDER.

On the two preceding pages we illustrate and present the principal particulars of the Six-Wheel Switching Locomotive, with tender, which is designed for switching service in yards and stations, and for short runs on local roads.

The weight of the engine is equally distributed among the six wheels, thus utilizing all the weight for adhesion, and there is an equalizing lever between the middle and back driving wheels on each side. There is also a transverse equalizing ever connecting the front ends of the forward springs.

The tender has either a straight or sloping top, and is provided with six wheels, or two four-wheeled trucks.

General specifications are given on the following page.

LOW MOOR IRON CO. OF VIRGINIA No. 2 – Dickson No. 412 – 1883

GENERAL SPECIFICATIONS.

BOILER.—Straight on top, or wagon top, as may be required. Smoke box made the usual length, using a bonnet or diamond smoke stack, or with an extension and spark arrester inside and a straight smoke stack. Material, best cold-blast charcoal iron, or all-guaranteed steel plate if required; all longitudinal seams on the larger boilers double riveted. Fire box of steel, of ample size for generating steam; tubes of best charcoal iron set with copper ferrules in both tube sheets; steam dome fitted with balanced throttle valve, one steam whistle and two safety valves of improved make; boiler furnished with steam gauge, blow-off cock, gauge cocks and blower valve, and covered with pine lagging and planished iron jacket; feed water supplied with one pump and one injector, or two injectors as required.

CYLINDERS.—Made of close-grained charcoal iron, as hard as can be worked, outside connected, horizontal, bolted together in center, right and left hand interchangeable heads, sides and steam chest furnished with iron casings.

PISTONS.—Steel rods, cast-iron heads and followers; packing rings of cast iron or brass.

CROSS HEADS—Of charcoal iron or cast steel.

GUIDE BARS—Of steel, or case-hardened iron, secured to wrought-iron yoke and cylinder head.

CONNECTING RODS.—Best quality hammered iron; boxes of best quality hard brass, lined with babbitt metal.

VALVE MOTION.—Shifting links of hammered iron, with all wearing parts bushed and case hardened; rocker shafts and lifting shafts of wrought iron with solid arms; cast-iron slide valves of the usual pattern.

DRIVING WHEELS.—Cast-iron centers; steel tires; hammered iron or steel axles as required; axle boxes of cast iron with cast brass bearings; crank pins of steel. Unless otherwise ordered on this class of locomotive we put flanges on all the wheels, but can make the middle pair of wheels with plain tires if required.

CAB—Of hard wood with plate-glass windows.

TANK—Of ample capacity, made straight on top with flanges on sides and back, or made sloping on back to give the engineer a clear view in the rear. Mounted on either an oak or an iron frame, with six wheels, or two four-wheel trucks; wheels double plate, chilled face, hammered iron axles with brass bearings.

TOOLS.—A complete set of iron and steel wrenches, one screw wrench, two chisels, hard hammers, two jack screws, one pinch bar and complete set of fire tools and set of oil cans.

MOUNTING, &c.—Running boards and hand rails on each side; one bell and frame; one or two sand boxes; brackets and shelf for head light; gauge lamp, and all necessary oil cups.

PAINTING.—Engine and tender neatly painted and varnished, and lettered and numbered to suit the purchaser.

"MOGUL" LOCOMOTIVE—FOR FREIGHT SERVICE.

CLASS E.

GAUGE, 4 FEET 8½ INCHES.

FUEL, ANTHRACITE COAL.

"MOGUL" LOCOMOTIVE—For Freight Service.

FUEL, ANTHRACITE COAL.
GAUGE, 4 FEET 8½ INCHES.

DIMENSIONS AND CAPACITIES OF NINE SIZES OF THIS CLASS.

CLASS	12-E	13-E	14-E	15-E	16-E	17-E	18-E	19-E	20-E
Cylinders, Diameter	12"	13"	14"	15"	16"	17"	18"	19"	20"
" Stroke	18" to 20"	18" to 20"	20" to 22"	20" to 22"	22" to 24"	22" to 24"	22" to 24"	22" to 24"	22" to 24"
Diameter of Driving Wheel	36" to 42"	36" to 42"	36" to 42"	40" to 44"	44" to 48"	46" to 56"	48" to 56"	54" to 60"	54" to 60"
" " Truck Wheel	24"	24"	26"	26"	28"	28"	30"	30"	30"
Wheel Base Rigid	9'-6"	10'-0"	10'-6"	11'-0"	12'-0"	13'-0"	14'-2"	14'-6"	15'-0"
" " Total	16'-0"	16'-6"	17'-4"	18'-2"	19'-4"	20'-6"	21'-8"	22'-0"	22'-6"
" " Engine and Tender	37'-6"	38'-0"	39'-6"	40'-0"	43'-0"	44'-4"	45'-5"	46'-5"	47'-5"
Length of Engine and Tender	46'-4"	46'-10"	49'-2"	49'-8"	52'-10"	54'-0"	55'-4"	56'-4"	57'-4"
Weight Loaded, Total	48,000 lbs.	53,000 lbs.	58,000 lbs.	64,000 lbs.	70,000 lbs.	77,000 lbs.	83,000 lbs.	90,000 lbs.	98,000 lbs.
" " on Drivers	40,000 lbs.	44,000 lbs.	48,000 lbs.	54,000 lbs.	59,000 lbs.	66,000 lbs.	71,000 lbs.	77,000 lbs.	85,000 lbs.
" " " Truck	8,000 lbs.	9,000 lbs.	10,000 lbs.	10,000 lbs.	11,000 lbs.	11,000 lbs.	12,000 lbs.	13,000 lbs.	13,000 lbs.
Capacity of Tank	1,400 gal.	1,500 gal.	1,800 gal.	2,000 gal.	2,000 gal.	2,400 gal.	2,600 gal.	2,800 gal.	3,000 gal.
Hauling Capacity on Level	985 tons.	1,085 tons.	1,180 tons.	1,325 tons.	1,450 tons.	1,625 tons.	1,750 tons.	1,895 tons.	2,095 tons.
" " 20 ft. Grade	470 "	520 "	560 "	630 "	690 "	775 "	835 "	900 "	1,000 "
" " 40 ft. "	310 "	340 "	370 "	410 "	455 "	510 "	550 "	595 "	660 "
" " 60 ft. "	225 "	250 "	270 "	300 "	330 "	370 "	400 "	435 "	480 "
" " 80 ft. "	175 "	195 "	210 "	230 "	255 "	290 "	315 "	340 "	375 "
" " 100 ft. "	145 "	160 "	170 "	190 "	210 "	235 "	255 "	275 "	305 "
Price ready for service on car at Scranton	$$	$$	$$	$$	$$	$$	$$	$$	$$

"Mogul" Locomotive.

CLASS E.

FOR ANTHRACITE COAL.

On the two preceding pages we give an illustration and table of principal particulars of the locomotive known as the "Mogul" (so called because the first one of its type was named "Mogul"), as built by us for burning anthracite coal.

Of late years this style of engine has come into use for heavy freight service, and weighs considerably more than the "American" type. The greater portion of its weight is carried on driving wheels, and as there are six of them, among which the weight is equally distributed, the pressure of each wheel on the rail is kept within a safe limit. The pilot truck is provided with a swing bolster and radius bar, which allows the engine to "take" curves with ease and safety even at high speeds, as is proved by their successful use for express passenger service in some instances. The weight on the truck is only sufficient to keep the engine securely on the track, and to gradually bring the rails down to the level to which they will be brought by the greater weight on the driving wheels. This is a matter of considerable importance, and is often overlooked. We build these engines with flanges on all the wheels, some of which have had fifteen feet of rigid wheel base, and after a year's service on a line having curves of ten degrees, show no appreciable signs of wear.

"Mogul" Engines for anthracite coal have the driving wheels equally spaced from each other, and in the larger sizes the fire box is placed above the frames, in order to have as large a grate area as possible without making the length of the fire box excessive.

We have made the building of the "Mogul" engine almost a specialty at our works, and recommend it as an economical type of engine for heavy service, and one which will do twenty-five per cent. more work than the "American" type for the same number of engine and train men.

On the following page are given general specifications of "Mogul" Engines, as we build them without special instructions.

DELAWARE & HUDSON CANAL CO. No. 201 *Guilderland* – Dickson No. 422 – 1883

GENERAL SPECIFICATIONS.

BOILER.—Made of best cold-blast charcoal plate iron, or all-guaranteed steel plate if required; longitudinal seams double riveted. Fire box of steel, tubes of best wrought iron set with copper ferrules at both ends; one-steam dome fitted with balanced throttle valve; one steam whistle and two safety valves; feed water supplied with one pump and one injector (or two injectors if required); boiler furnished with steam gauge, blow-off cock, gauge cocks and blower valve, and covered with pine lagging and planished iron jacket.

CYLINDERS.—Made of close-grained charcoal iron, as hard as can be worked, outside connected, horizontal, bolted together in center, right and left hand interchangeable, heads, sides and steam chest furnished with iron casings.

PISTONS.—Steel rods, cast-iron heads and followers; packing rings of cast iron or brass.

CROSS HEADS—Of charcoal iron or cast steel.

GUIDE BARS—Of steel, or case-hardened iron, secured to wrought-iron yoke and cylinder head.

CONNECTING RODS.—Best quality hammered iron; boxes of best quality hard brass, lined with babbitt metal.

VALVE MOTION.—Shifting links of hammered iron, case hardened, with all wearing parts bushed and case hardened; rocker shafts and lifting shaft of wrought iron, with solid arms; cast-iron slide valves of the usual pattern.

DRIVING WHEELS.—Cast-iron centers; steel tires; hammered iron or steel axles as required; axle boxes of cast iron with brass bearings; crank pins of steel.

ENGINE TRUCK.—Swing bolster, with radius bar; chilled wheels; hammered iron axles; cast-iron axle boxes with brass bearings.

CAB—Of hard wood with plate-glass windows.

PILOT—Of hard wood or wrought iron.

TANK.—Mounted on either an oak or, an iron frame, with two four-wheeled trucks; wheels double plate, chilled face; hammered iron axles with brass bearings.

TOOLS.—A complete set of iron and steel wrenches, one screw wrench, two chisels, hard and soft hammers, two jack screws, one pinch bar, and complete set of fire tools and set of oil cans.

MOUNTING, &c.—Running boards and hand rails on each side; one bell and frame; one sand box; brackets and shelf for head light; signal gong; gauge lamp, and all necessary oil cups.

"MOGUL" LOCOMOTIVE—FOR FREIGHT SERVICE.

CLASS E.

GAUGE, 4 FEET 8½ INCHES.

FUEL, BITUMINOUS COAL, OR WOOD.

"MOGUL" LOCOMOTIVE—For FREIGHT SERVICE.

FUEL, BITUMINOUS COAL, OR WOOD.
GAUGE, 4 FEET 8½ INCHES.

DIMENSIONS AND CAPACITIES OF EIGHT SIZES OF THIS CLASS

CLASS	12-E	13-E	14-E	15-E	16-E	17-E	18-E	19-E
Cylinders, Diameter	12"	18"	14"	15"	16"	17"	18"	19"
" Stroke	18" to 20"	18" to 20"	20" to 22"	20" to 22"	22" to 24"	22" to 24"	22" to 24"	22" to 24"
Diameter of Driving Wheel	36" to 42"	36" to 42"	36" to 42"	40" to 44"	44" to 48"	48" to 56"	54" to 60"	54" to 60"
" " Truck Wheel	24"	24"	26"	26"	28"	28" to 30"	30"	30"
Wheel Base Rigid	12'-0"	12'-6"	18'-0"	12'-6"	14'-0"	14'-6"	15'-0"	15'-2"
" " Total	18'-6"	19'-0"	19'-10"	20'-8"	21'-4"	22'-0"	22'-6"	22'-10"
" " Engine and Tender	37'-8"	38'-4"	39'-5"	40'-8"	40'-11"	41'-7"	43'-1"	43'-5"
Length of Engine and Tender	46'-8"	47'-2"	48'-9"	49'-11"	50'-7"	51'-6"	58'-0"	58'-4"
Weight Loaded, Total	47,000 lbs.	52,000 lbs.	57,000 lbs.	62,000 lbs.	68,000 lbs.	75,000 lbs.	80,000 lbs.	86,000 lbs.
" " on Drivers	39,000 lbs.	48,000 lbs.	47,000 lbs.	52,000 lbs.	57,000 lbs.	64,000 lbs.	68,000 lbs.	73,000 lbs.
" " " Truck	8,000 lbs.	9,000 lbs.	10,000 lbs.	10,000 lbs.	11,000 lbs.	11,000 lbs.	12,000 lbs.	12,000 lbs.
Capacity of Tank	1,400 gal.	1,500 gal.	1,800 gal.	2,000 gal.	2,000 gal.	2,400 gal.	2,600 gal.	2,800 gal.
Hauling Capacity on Level	960 tons.	1,060 tons.	1,155 tons.	1,275 tons.	1,400 tons.	1,575 tons.	1,675 tons.	1,795 tons.
" " 20 ft. Grade	460	505	550	605	665	750	795	855
" " 40 ft. "	300	385	360	385	435	495	525	561
" " 60 ft. "	220	245	260	285	315	360	385	410
" " 80 ft. "	170	190	205	225	245	280	300	320
" " 100 ft. "	140	155	165	180	200	280	245	260
Price ready for service on car at Scranton	$	$	$	$	$	$	$	$

"Mogul" Locomotive.

CLASS E.

FOR BITUMINOUS COAL, OR WOOD.

The two preceding pages we devote to a representation and table of principal dimensions and hauling capacities of a number of sizes of this engine as built by us for burning bituminous coal or wood.

The remarks on page 54 apply to this locomotive, except those which refer to the peculiarities of construction of the fire box and the spacing of the driving wheels. In the bituminous coal burning "Mogul" the fire box is placed between the two back pairs of driving-wheel axles, which causes their unequal spacing.

ST. LOUIS COAL RAILROAD No. 8 – Dickson No. 342 – 1882

GENERAL SPECIFICATIONS.

BOILER.—Made of best cold-blast charcoal plate iron, or all-guaranteed steel plate if required; longitudinal seams double riveted. Fire box of steel, tubes of best wrought iron set with copper ferrules at both ends; one steam dome fitted with balanced throttle valve; one steam whistle and two safety valves; feed water supplied with one pump and one injector (or two injectors if required); boiler furnished with steam gauge, blow-off cock, gauge cocks and blower valve, and covered with pine lagging and planished iron jacket.

CYLINDERS.—Made of close-grained charcoal iron, as hard as can be worked, outside connected, horizontal, bolted together in center, right and left hand interchangeable, heads, sides and steam chest furnished with iron casings.

PISTONS.—Steel rods, cast-iron heads and followers; packing rings of cast iron or brass.

CROSS HEADS—Of charcoal iron or cast steel.

GUIDE BARS—Of steel, or case-hardened iron, secured to wrought-iron yoke and cylinder head.

CONNECTING RODS.—Best quality hammered iron; boxes of best quality hard brass, lined with babbitt metal.

VALVE MOTION.—Shifting links of hammered iron, case hardened, with all wearing parts bushed and case hardened; rocker shafts and lifting shaft of wrought iron, with solid arms; cast-iron slide valves of the usual pattern.

DRIVING WHEELS.—Cast-iron centers; steel tires; hammered iron or steel axles, if required; axle boxes of cast iron with brass bearings; crank pins of steel.

ENGINE TRUCK.—Swing bolster, with radius bar; chilled wheels; hammered iron axles; cast-iron axle boxes with brass bearings.

CAB—Of hard wood with plate-glass windows.

PILOT—Of hard wood or wrought iron.

TANK.—Mounted on either an oak or an iron frame, with two four-wheeled trucks; wheels double plate, chilled face; hammered iron axles with brass bearings.

TOOLS.—A complete set of iron and steel wrenches, one screw wrench, two chisels, hard and soft hammers, two jack screws, one pinch bar, and complete set of fire tools and set of oil cans.

MOUNTING, &c.—Running boards and hand rails on each side; one bell and frame; one sand box; brackets and shelf for head light; signal gong; gauge lamp, and all necessary oil cups.

SIX WHEELS COUPLED SWITCHING LOCOMOTIVE.

CLASS E.

GAUGE, 4 FEET 8½ INCHES.

FUEL, COAL OR WOOD.

SIX WHEELS COUPLED SWITCHING LOCOMOTIVE.

GAUGE, 4 FEET 8½ INCHES. FUEL, COAL OR WOOD.

DIMENSIONS AND CAPACITIES OF SIX SIZES OF THIS CLASS.

CLASS	14—E	15—E	16—E	17—E	18—E	19—E
Cylinders, Diameter	14″	15″	16″	17″	18″	19″
" Stroke	22″	22″	22″ or 24″	22″ or 24″	22″ or 24″	22″ or 24″
Diameter of Driving Wheels	40″ to 50″	42″ to 54″	42″ to 54″	42″ to 54″	44″ to 56″	44″ to 56″
" Truck Wheels	25″ to 30″	26″ to 30″	26″ to 30″	26″ to 30″	28″ to 30″	28″ to 30″
Wheel Base, Rigid	9' 9″	10' 0″	10' 0″	10' 3″	10' 6″	10' 9″
" " Total	16' 10″	17' 3″	17' 6″	17' 10″	18' 4″	18' 10″
Length of Engine without Pilot	28' 0″	28' 9″	29' 6″	30' 0″	31' 0″	32' 0″
" " with one Pilot	31' 0″	32' 0″	32' 9″	33' 6″	34' 6″	35' 6″
Weight, Loaded, Total	68,000 lbs.	74,000 lbs.	80,000 lbs.	86,000 lbs.	92,000 lbs.	98,000 lbs.
" " on Drivers	56,000 "	62,000 "	67,000 "	73,000 "	78,000 "	84,000 "
" " on Trucks	12,000 "	12,000 "	13,000 "	13,000 "	14,000 "	14,000 "
Capacity of Tank	700 gal.	750 gal.	850 gal.	900 gal.	950 gal.	1,000 gal.
Hauling Capacity on Level	1,800 tons.	1,425 tons.	1,575 tons.	1,700 tons.	1,825 tons.	1,950 tons.
" " 20 ft. Grade	625 "	685 "	760 "	820 "	830 "	940 "
" " 40 ft. "	420 "	460 "	510 "	550 "	590 "	630 "
" " 60 ft. "	310 "	340 "	375 "	405 "	430 "	465 "
" " 80 ft. "	245 "	270 "	305 "	320 "	345 "	370 "
" " 100 ft. "	206 "	225 "	245 "	265 "	285 "	305 "
Prices ready for service at works in Scranton	$	$	$	$	$	$

Six Wheels Coupled Tank Locomotive.

CLASS E.

On the preceding page we present the general dimensions, weights and hauling capacities of several sizes of the six-coupled "Tank Switching" Locomotive, pony truck. This is designed for switching service, or for very short runs in the suburban service of cities or for logging service. It is also well adapted to elevated railroads, as it runs steadily and passes with ease around curves of short radius.

GENERAL SPECIFICATIONS.

BOILER.—Made of best cold-blast charcoal plate iron, or all-guaranteed steel plate if required; longitudinal seams double riveted in the larger sizes. Fire box of steel, tubes of best wrought iron set with copper ferrules at both ends; one steam dome fitted with balanced throttle valve; one steam whistle and two safety valves; feed water supplied with one pump and one injector (or two injectors if required); boiler furnished with steam gauge, blow-off cock, gauge cocks and blower valve, and covered with pine lagging and planished iron jacket.

CYLINDERS.—Made of close-grained charcoal iron, as hard as can be worked, outside connected, horizontal, bolted together in center, right and left hand interchangeable, heads, sides and steam chest furnished with iron casings.

PISTONS.—Steel rods, cast-iron heads and followers; packing rings of cast iron or brass.

CROSS HEADS—Of charcoal iron or cast steel.

GUIDE BARS—Of steel, or case-hardened iron, secured to wrought-iron yoke and cylinder head.

CONNECTING RODS.—Best quality hammered iron; boxes of best quality hard brass, lined with babbitt metal.

VALVE MOTION.—Shifting links of hammered iron, case hardened, with all wearing parts bushed and case hardened; rocker shafts and lifting shaft of wrought iron, with solid arms; cast-iron slide valves of the usual pattern.

DRIVING WHEELS.—Cast-iron centers; steel tires; hammered iron or steel axles as required; axle boxes, cast iron with brass bearings; crank pins of steel.

TRUCK.—Swing bolster, with radius bar, equalized with driving wheels; chilled wheels; hammered iron axles; cast-iron axle boxes with brass bearings.

CAB—Of hard wood with plate-glass windows.

TANK.—Mounted on top of boiler.

TOOLS.—A complete set of iron and steel wrenches, one screw wrench, two chisels, hard and soft hammers, two jack screws, one pinch bar, and complete set of fire tools and set of oil cans.

MOUNTING, &c.—Running boards and hand rails on each side; one bell and frame; one sand box; brackets and shelf for head light; signal gong; gauge lamp, and all necessary oil cups.

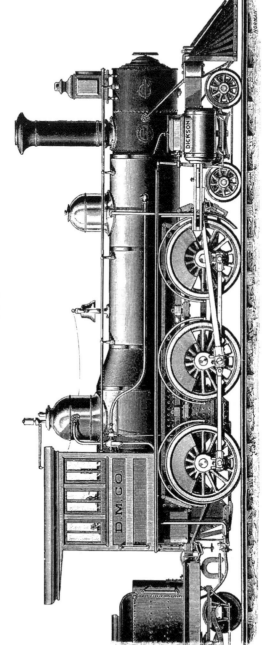

"Ten-Wheel" Freight Locomotive.

CLASS F.

Gauge, 4 Feet 8½ Inches.

FUEL, ANTHRACITE COAL.

"TEN-WHEEL" FREIGHT LOCOMOTIVE.

GAUGE, 4 FEET 8½ INCHES.   FUEL, ANTHRACITE COAL.

DIMENSIONS AND CAPACITIES OF SIX SIZES OF THIS CLASS.

CLASS	15—F	16—F	17—F	18—F	19—F	20—F
Cylinders, Diameter	15"	16"	17"	18"	19"	20"
" Stroke	20" to 22"	22" to 24"	22" to 24"	22" to 24"	22" to 24"	22" to 24"
Diameter of Driving Wheels	40" to 44"	44" to 48"	48" to 56"	48" to 56"	54" to 60"	54" to 60"
" Truck "	22" to 24"	24" to 26"	26" to 28"	26" to 28"	28" to 30"	28" to 30"
Wheel Base, Rigid	9' 6"	10' 0"	11' 0"	12' 0"	13' 0"	13' 0"
" " Total	19' 0"	19' 10"	21' 1"	22' 1"	23' 3"	23' 3"
" " Engine and Tender	40' 4"	41' 2"	43' 4"	45' 2"	47' 7"	47' 7"
Length of " "	49' 0"	50' 0"	52' 2"	53' 0"	56' 5"	56' 5"
Weight Loaded, Total	66,000 lbs.	73,000 lbs.	79,000 lbs.	85,000 lbs.	92,000 lbs.	100,000 lbs.
" on Drivers	50,000 "	55,000 "	60,000 "	65,000 "	71,000 "	78,000 "
" on Truck	16,000 "	18,000 "	19,000 "	20,000 "	21,000 "	22,000 "
Capacity of Tank	2,000 gal.	2,200 gal.	2,400 gal.	2,600 gal.	2,800 gal.	3,000 gal.
Hauling Capacity on Level	1,230 tons.	1,325 tons.	1,475 tons.	1,600 tons.	1,750 tons.	1,920 tons.
" " 20 ft. Grade	585 "	630 "	705 "	760 "	835 "	915 "
" " 40 ft. "	385 "	410 "	460 "	500 "	550 "	605 "
" " 60 ft. "	280 "	300 "	335 "	385 "	400 "	440 "
" " 80 ft. "	220 "	230 "	260 "	285 "	315 "	345 "
" " 100 ft. "	180 "	190 "	210 "	230 "	255 "	280 "
Prices ready for service at works in Scranton	$	$	$	$	$	$

Ten-Wheel Locomotive.

CLASS F.

FOR ANTHRACITE COAL.

On the two preceding pages we present the general dimensions, weights and hauling capacities of several of the more common sizes of the so-called Ten-Wheel Freight Locomotive, which is extensively used on American railroads, and will do twenty per cent. more work with the same number of engine and train men than the " American " type.

The driving wheels of the Ten-Wheel Locomotive are so placed as to utilize most of the weight for adhesion, and as it is equally distributed among them, it is not so severe on the track as the " American " type of the same weight, although the latter is generally much lighter than the former. On the larger sizes of this engine, when built for burning anthracite coal, the fire box is placed above the frames, by means of which construction it can be made eight or nine inches wider than when placed between them. The grate area is thus increased some twenty-five per cent., and the steaming capacity of the engine thereby benefited. The truck has four wheels, and is made either with or without a swing bolster.

The general specifications, as we usually build this engine, follow.

GENERAL SPECIFICATIONS.

BOILER.—Wagon top plain with one dome, or made straight on top with one dome in center, or two domes, as may be required. Smoke box made the usual length, using a bonnet or diamond smoke stack, or with an extension and spark arrester inside and a straight smoke stack. Material, best cold-blast charcoal iron, or all-guaranteed steel plate if required; all longitudinal seams double riveted. Fire box of steel, of ample size for generating steam; flues of best charcoal iron set with copper ferrules in both flue heads; steam dome fitted with balanced throttle valve, one steam whistle and two safety valves of improved make; boiler furnished with steam gauge, blow-off cock, gauge cocks and blower valve, and covered with pine lagging and planished iron jacket; feed water supplied with one pump and one injector, or two injectors if required.

CYLINDERS.—Made of close-grained charcoal iron, as hard as can be worked, outside connected, horizontal, bolted together in center, right and left hand interchangeable, heads, sides and steam chest furnished with iron casings.

PISTONS.—Steel rods, cast-iron heads and followers; packing rings of cast iron or brass.

CROSS HEADS—Of charcoal iron or cast steel.

GUIDE BARS—Of steel secured to wrought-iron yoke and cylinder head.

CONNECTING RODS.—Best quality hammered iron; boxes of best quality hard brass, lined with babbitt metal.

VALVE MOTION.—Shifting links of hammered iron, with all wearing parts bushed and case hardened; rocker shafts and lifting shafts of wrought iron, with solid arms; cast-iron slide valves of the usual pattern.

DRIVING WHEELS.—Cast-iron centers; steel tires; hammered iron or steel axles as required; axle boxes of cast iron with cast brass bearings; crank pins of steel. Unless otherwise ordered on this class of locomotive we put flanges on all the wheels, but will make either the middle pair or the front pair with plain tires if required. If the front pair of driving wheels are made with plain tires we would recommend a truck with center bearings

ENGINE TRUCK.—Center bearing or swing bolster, with chilled wheels; hammered iron axles; cast-iron axle boxes with brass bearings.

CAB—Of hard wood with plate-glass windows.

PILOT—Of hard wood or wrought iron.

TANK.—Mounted on either an oak or an iron frame, with two four-wheeled trucks; wheels double plate, chilled face; hammered iron axles with brass bearings.

TOOLS.—A complete set of iron and steel wrenches, one screw wrench, two chisels, hard and soft hammers, two jack screws, one pinch bar, and complete set of fire tools and set of oil cans.

MOUNTING, &c.—Running boards and hand rails on each side; one bell and frame; one sand box; brackets and shelf for head light; signal gong; gauge lamp and all necessary oil cups.

PAINTING.—Engine and tender neatly painted and varnished, and lettered and numbered to suit purchaser.

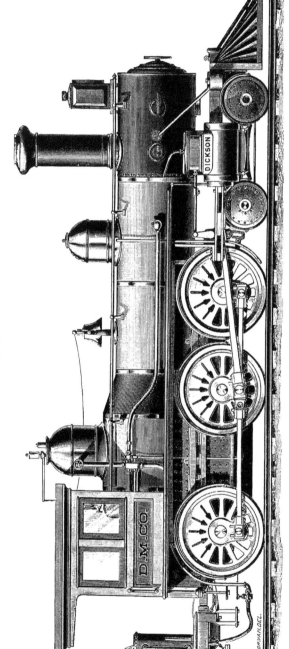

"TEN-WHEEL" FREIGHT LOCOMOTIVE.

CLASS F.

GAUGE, 4 FEET 8½ INCHES.

FUEL, BITUMINOUS COAL, OR WOOD.

"Ten-Wheel" Freight Locomotive.

GAUGE, 4 FEET 8½ INCHES.   FUEL, BITUMINOUS COAL, OR WOOD.

DIMENSIONS AND CAPACITIES OF FIVE SIZES OF THIS CLASS.

CLASS	15–F	16–F	17–F	18–F	19–F
Cylinders, Diameter	15"	16"	17"	18"	19"
" Stroke	22" to 24"	22" to 24"	22" to 24"	22" to 24"	22" to 24"
Diameter of Driving Wheels	40" to 44"	44" to 48"	48" to 56"	48" to 56"	54" to 60"
" Truck Wheels	22" to 24"	24" to 26"	26" to 28"	26" to 28"	28" to 30"
Wheel Base, Rigid	11' 9"	12' 4"	12' 11"	13' 2"	13' 10"
" " Total	21' 3"	22' 2"	23' 0"	23' 3"	24' 1"
" " Engine and Tender	40' 10"	41' 9"	42' 7"	43' 10"	44' 8"
Length of " "	49' 6"	50' 7"	51' 5"	52' 8"	53' 6"
Weight Loaded, Total	64,000 lbs.	70,000 lbs.	76,000 lbs.	82,000 lbs.	88,000 lbs.
" on Drivers	47,000 "	51,000 "	56,000 "	61,000 "	66,000 "
" on Truck	17,000 "	19,000 "	20,000 "	21,000 "	22,000 "
Capacity of Tank	2,000 gal.	2,200 gal.	2,400 gal.	2,600 gal.	2,800 gal.
Hauling Capacity on Level	1,155 tons.	1,250 tons.	1,375 tons	1,500 tons.	1,625 tons.
" 20 ft. Grade	550 "	590 "	655 "	715 "	775 "
" 40 ft. "	360 "	390 "	430 "	470 "	510 "
" 60 ft. "	260 "	280 "	310 "	340 "	370 "
" 80 ft. "	205 "	215 "	240 "	285 "	290 "
" 100 ft. "	165 "	175 "	195 "	215 "	235 "
Prices ready for service at works in Scranton	$	$	$	$	$

Ten-Wheel Locomotive.

CLASS F.

FOR BITUMINOUS COAL, OR WOOD.

On the two preceding pages we give particulars of our Ten-Wheel Locomotives, as we build them for burning bituminous coal, or wood.

The description of the same class of engine given on page 66 applies here, except that in the case of the bituminous coal burning engine, the fire box is always between the frames and between the two back driving-wheel axles, causing the unequal spacing of the wheels.

Specifications are given on the following page.

GENERAL SPECIFICATIONS.

BOILER.—Wagon top plain with one dome, or made straight on top with one dome in center, or two domes, as may be required. Smoke box made the usual length, using a bonnet or diamond smoke stack, or with an extension and spark arrester inside and a straight smoke stack. Material, best cold-blast charcoal iron, or all-guaranteed steel plate if required; all longitudinal seams double riveted. Fire box of steel, of ample size for generating steam; flues of best charcoal iron set with copper ferrules in both flue heads; steam dome fitted with balanced throttle valve; one steam whistle and two safety valves of improved make; boiler furnished with steam gauge, blow-off cock, gauge cocks and blower valve, and covered with pine lagging and planished iron jacket; feed water supplied with one pump and one injector, or two injectors if required.

CYLINDERS.—Made of close-grained charcoal iron, as hard as can be worked, outside connected, horizontal, bolted together in center, right and left hand interchangeable, heads, sides and steam chest furnished with iron casings.

PISTONS.—Steel rods, cast-iron heads and followers; packing rings of cast iron or brass.

CROSS HEADS—Of charcoal iron or cast steel.

GUIDE BARS—Of steel, secured to wrought-iron yoke and cylinder head.

CONNECTING RODS.—Best quality hammered iron; boxes of best quality hard brass, lined with babbitt metal.

VALVE MOTION.—Shifting links of hammered iron, with all wearing parts bushed and case hardened; rocker shafts and lifting shafts of wrought iron, with solid arms; cast-iron slide valves of the usual pattern.

DRIVING WHEELS.—Cast-iron centers; steel tires; hammered iron or steel axles as required; axle boxes of cast iron with cast brass bearings; crank pins of steel. Unless otherwise ordered on this class of locomotive we put flanges on all the wheels, but will make either the middle pair or the front pair with plain tires if required. If the front pair of driving wheels are made with plain tires we would recommend a truck with center bearings.

ENGINE TRUCK.—Center bearing or swing bolster, with chilled wheels; hammered iron axles; cast-iron axle boxes with brass bearings.

CAB—Of hard wood with plate-glass windows.

PILOT—Of hard wood or wrought iron.

TANK.—Mounted on either an oak or an iron frame, with two four-wheeled trucks; wheels double plate, chilled face; hammered iron axles with brass bearings.

TOOLS.—A complete set of iron and steel wrenches, one screw wrench, two chisels, hard and soft hammers, two jack screws, one pinch bar, and complete set of fire tools and set of oil cans.

MOUNTING, &c.—Running boards and hand rails on each side; one bell and frame; one sand box; brackets and shelf for head light; signal gong; gauge lamp, and all necessary oil cups.

PAINTING.—Engine and tender neatly painted and varnished, and lettered and numbered to suit the purchaser.

"CONSOLIDATION" LOCOMOTIVE.

CLASS H.

GAUGE, 4 FEET 8½ INCHES.

FUEL, ANTHRACITE OR BITUMINOUS COAL, OR WOOD.

NEW YORK, WEST SHORE & BUFFALO No. 158 – Dickson No. 368 – 1883

"CONSOLIDATION" LOCOMOTIVE.

GAUGE, 4 FEET 8½ INCHES.   FUEL, ANTHRACITE OR BITUMINOUS COAL, OR WOOD.

DIMENSIONS AND CAPACITIES OF FIVE SIZES OF THIS CLASS.

CLASS	18—H	19—H	20—H	21—H	22—H
Cylinders, Diameter	18″	19″	20″	21″	22″
" Stroke	24″	24″	24″	24″ or 26″	24″ or 26″
Diameter of Driving Wheels	50″	50″	50″	50″	50″
" Truck Wheels	30″	30″	30″	30″	30″
Wheel Base, Rigid	14′ 9″	14′ 9″	15′ 0″	15′ 0″	15′ 0″
" " Total	22′ 10″	22′ 10″	23′ 1″	23′ 1″	23′ 1″
" " Engine and Tender	45′ 7″	46′ 1″	46′ 7″	46′ 7″	47′ 10″
Length of " " "	53′ 9″	55′ 8″	56′ 2″	56′ 3″	57′ 6″
Weight, Loaded, Total	88,000 lbs.	95,000 lbs.	103,000 lbs.	114,000 lbs.	125,000 lbs.
" " on Drivers	76,000 "	82,000 "	90,000 "	100,000 "	110,000 "
" " on Truck	12,000 "	13,000 "	13,000 "	14,000 "	15,000 "
Capacity of Tank	2,400 gal.	2,600 gal.	2,800 gal.	3,000 gal.	3,000 gal.
Hauling Capacity on Level	1,875 tons.	2,025 tons.	2,225 tons.	2,470 tons.	2,720 tons.
" " 20 ft. Grade	895 "	965 "	1,060 "	1,180 "	1,300 "
" " 40 ft. "	590 "	640 "	700 "	780 "	860 "
" " 60 ft. "	430 "	465 "	510 "	570 "	680 "
" " 80 ft. "	338 "	365 "	400 "	450 "	495 "
" " 100 ft. "	275 "	300 "	330 "	370 "	405 "
Prices ready for service at works in Scranton	$	$	$	$	$

Consolidation Locomotive.

CLASS H.

On the two preceding pages we give the leading particulars of the " Consolidation " Locomotive (which received its name from that of the first one built), which is now in common use for very heavy freight service, and as helpers or pushers on heavy grades. It is the heaviest type commonly built, is the most economical for the service for which it is designed, and will do from forty to fifty per cent. more work with the same number of engine and train men than the "American " type.

There are eight coupled wheels, and a two-wheeled pilot truck in front with a swinging bolster or center, and a radius bar of the proper length to allow the engine to pass easily around curves. We have built such engines having fifteen feet of rigid wheel base with flanges on all the wheels, which after a year's service on a line having curves of ten degrees, show no appreciable signs of wear on the flanges. On the larger sizes we make the boiler with the fire box on top of the frames, in order to gain eight or nine inches in width, and thus increase the grate area some twenty-five per cent., which is essential for free steaming. The boilers are made either straight or wagon top, with or without the extended smoke box, and with a grate either for anthracite or bituminous coal.

On the following page are given general specifications as we generally build these locomotives.

GENERAL SPECIFICATIONS.

BOILER.—Wagon top plain with one dome, or straight on top with one dome in center, or two domes, as may be required. Smoke box made the usual length, using a bonnet or diamond smoke stack, or with an extension and spark arrester inside and a straight smoke stack. Material, best cold-blast charcoal iron, or all-guaranteed steel plate if required; all longitudinal seams double riveted. Fire box of steel, of ample size for generating steam (see preceding page for fire box); tubes of best charcoal iron set with copper ferrules in both tube heads; steam dome fitted with balanced throttle valve, one steam whistle and two safety valves of improved make; boiler furnished with steam gauge, blow-off cock, gauge cocks and blower valve, and covered with pine lagging and planished iron jacket; feed water supplied with one pump and one injector, or two injectors if required.

CYLINDERS.—Made of close-grained charcoal iron, as hard as can be worked, outside connected, horizontal, bolted together in center, right and left hand interchangeable, heads, sides and steam chest furnished with iron casings.

PISTONS.—Steel rods, cast-iron heads and followers; packing rings of cast iron or brass.

CROSS HEADS—Of wrought iron or cast steel.

GUIDE BARS—Of steel, secured to wrought-iron yoke and cylinder head.

CONNECTING RODS.—Best quality hammered iron; boxes of best quality hard brass, lined with babbitt metal.

VALVE MOTION.—Shifting links of hammered iron, with all wearing parts bushed and case hardened; rocker shafts and lifting shafts of wrought iron, with solid arms; cast-iron slide valves of the usual pattern.

DRIVING WHEELS.—Cast-iron centers; steel tires; hammered iron or steel axles, as required; axle boxes of cast iron with cast brass bearings; crank pins of steel. Unless otherwise ordered on this class of locomotive we put flanges on all the wheels, but will make the first and third pairs or the second and third pairs of wheels with plain tires if required (see preceding page for flanged tires and wheel base).

ENGINE TRUCK.—Swing bolster, with radius bar; hammered iron axles; cast-iron axle boxe with cast brass bearings.

CAB—Of hard wood with plate-glass windows.

PILOT—Of hard wood or wrought iron.

TANK.—Mounted on either an oak or an iron frame, with two four-wheeled trucks; wheels double plate, chilled face; hammered iron axles with brass bearings.

TOOLS.—A complete set of iron and steel wrenches, one screw wrench, two chisels, hard and soft hammers, two jack screws, one pinch bar, and complete set of fire tools and set of oil cans.

MOUNTING, &c.—Running boards and hand rails on each side; one bell and frame; one sand box; brackets and shelf for head light; signal gong; gauge lamp, and all necessary oil cups.

PAINTING.—Engine and tender neatly painted and varnished, and lettered and numbered to suit the purchaser.

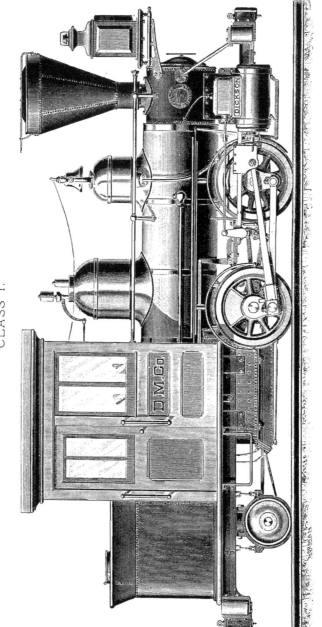

SWITCHING ENGINE—WITH TANK.

CLASS I.

GAUGE, 4 FEET 8½ INCHES.

FUEL, COAL OR WOOD.

SWITCHING ENGINE—WITH TANK.

GAUGE, 4 FEET 8½ INCHES.   FUEL, COAL OR WOOD.

DIMENSIONS AND CAPACITIES OF EIGHT SIZES OF THIS CLASS.

CLASS	10—1	11—1	12—1	13—1	14—1	15—1	16—1	17—1
Cylinders, Diameter	10"	11"	12"	13"	14"	15"	16"	17"
" Stroke	16"	16"	18"	20"	22"	22"	22" or 24"	22" or 24"
Diameter of Driving Wheels	33" to 40"	36" to 42"	36" to 45"	36" to 48"	40" to 50"	42" to 54"	42" to 54"	44" to 56"
" Truck Wheels	22" to 24"	24" to 26"	24" to 26"	24" to 28"	26" to 30'	26" to 30"	26" to 30"	28" to 30"
Wheel Base, Rigid	5' 8"	5' 6"	5' 9"	6' 0"	6' 6"	7' 0"	7' 6"	7' 6"
" Total	12' 0"	12' 9"	13' 6"	14' 3"	15' 3"	16' 0"	17' 0"	17' 6"
Length of Engine without Pilot	22' 6"	23' 6"	24' 9"	26' 3"	27' 6"	28' 6"	29' 9"	30' 3"
" with one Pilot	25' 2"	26' 6"	27' 9"	29' 6"	30' 0"	31' 9"	33' 0"	33' 6"
Weight, Loaded, Total	34,000 lbs.	40,000 lbs.	46,000 lbs.	52,000 lbs.	58,000 lbs.	64,000 lbs.	70,000 lbs.	76,000 lbs.
" on Drivers	26,000 "	31,000 "	36,000 "	42,000 "	47,000 "	53,000 "	58,000 "	64,000 "
" on Truck	8,000 "	9,000 "	10,000 "	10,000 "	11,000 "	11,000 "	12,000 "	12,000 "
Capacity of Tank	450 gal.	500 gal.	550 gal.	600 gal.	650 gal.	750 gal.	850 gal.	950 gal.
Hauling Capacity on Level	600 tons.	725 tons.	850 tons.	975 tons.	1,100 tons.	1,250 tons.	1,400 tons.	1,550 tons.
" 20 ft. Grade	290 "	850 "	410 "	460 "	530 "	605 "	680 "	750 "
" 40 ft. "	195 "	285 "	275 "	315 "	355 "	405 "	455 "	500 "
" 60 ft. "	145 "	175 "	205 "	235 "	265 "	300 "	335 "	370 "
" 80 ft. "	115 "	140 "	160 "	185 "	210 "	240 "	265 "	295 "
" 100 ft. "	95 "	115 "	135 "	160 "	175 "	200 "	220 "	245 "
Prices ready for service at works in Scranton	🙶	🙶	🙶	🙶	🙶	🙶	🙶	🙶

Tank Switching Engine.

CLASS I.

The Class " I " Tank Switching Locomotive, of which we present particulars, is made with the tank as shown on the engraving, or on top of the boiler, and is designed for switching, or for logging or plantation service. The rear truck, which is used whether the tank is on the boiler or not, is of the swing-bolster, radius-bar kind, and has a general steadying effect upon the engine when in motion.

General specifications are given on the next page.

GENERAL SPECIFICATIONS.

BOILER.—Made of best cold-blast charcoal plate iron, or all-guaranteed steel plate if required ; longitudinal seams double riveted for the larger sizes. Fire box of steel, tubes of best wrought iron set with copper ferrules at both ends ; one steam dome fitted with balanced throttle valve ; one steam whistle and two safety valves ; feed water supplied with one pump and one injector (or two injectors if required) ; boiler furnished with steam gauge, blow-off cock, gauge cocks and blower valve, and covered with pine lagging and planished iron jacket.

CYLINDERS.—Made of close-grained charcoal iron, as hard as can be worked, outside connected, horizontal, bolted together in center, right and left hand interchangeable, heads, sides and steam chest furnished with iron casings.

PISTONS.—Steel rods, cast-iron heads and followers ; packing rings of cast iron or brass.

CROSS HEADS—Of charcoal iron or cast steel.

GUIDE BARS—Of steel, or case-hardened iron, secured to wrought-iron yoke and cylinder head.

CONNECTING RODS.—Best quality hammered iron ; boxes of best quality hard brass, lined with babbitt metal.

VALVE MOTION.—Shifting links of hammered iron, with all wearing parts bushed and case hardened ; rocker shafts and lifting shaft of wrought iron, with solid arms ; cast-iron slide valves of the usual pattern.

DRIVING WHEELS.—Cast-iron centers ; steel tires ; hammered iron or steel axles if required ; axle boxes, cast iron with brass bearings ; crank pins of steel.

TRUCK.—Swing bolster, with radius bar ; chilled wheels ; hammered iron axles ; cast-iron axle boxes with brass bearings.

CAB—Of hard wood with plate-glass windows.

TANK.—Mounted on top of boiler or over truck.

TOOLS.—A complete set of iron and steel wrenches, one screw wrench, two chisels, hard and soft hammers, two jack screws, one pinch bar, and complete set of fire tools and set of oil cans.

MOUNTING, &c.—Running boards and hand rails on each side ; one bell and frame ; one sand box ; brackets and shelf for head light ; signal gong ; gauge lamp, and all necessary oil cups.

DOUBLE-ENDER LOCOMOTIVE—FOR SWITCHING OR SUBURBAN SERVICE.

CLASS J.

GAUGE, 4 FEET 8½ INCHES.

FUEL, COAL OR WOOD.

DOUBLE-ENDER LOCOMOTIVE—FOR SWITCHING OR SUBURBAN SERVICE.

GAUGE, 4 FEET 8½ INCHES.   FUEL, COAL OR WOOD.

DIMENSIONS AND CAPACITIES OF EIGHT SIZES OF THIS CLASS.

CLASS	10—J	11—J	12—J	13—J	14—J	15—J	16—J	17—J
Cylinders, Diameter	10"	11"	12"	13"	14"	15"	16"	17"
" Stroke	16"	16'	18"	20"	20" or 22"	20" or 22"	22" or 24"	22" or 24"
Diameter of Driving Wheels	37½" to 42"	37½" to 42"	40" to 48"	40" to 48"	42" to 50"	44" to 58"	45' to 58"	50" to 60"
" Truck Wheels	24"	24" to 28"	24" to 26"	24" to 26"	24" to 28"	26" to 28"	26" to 30"	26" to 30"
Wheel Base, Rigid	5' 8"	5' 6"	5' 9"	6 ft.	6' 6"	7 ft.	7' 6"	7' 6"
" " Total	17' 6½"	18' 2½"	19' 1½"	20' ½"	21' 2"	22' 3"	23' 4"	23' 9"
Length of Engine without Pilots	28' ½"	23' 8½"	24' 11½"	25' 11"	27' ½"	28' 3"	29' 4"	29' 9"
" with Pilots	28' ½"	29' 2½"	30' 5½"	31' 11"	33' ½"	34' 9"	35' 10"	36' 3"
Weight, Loaded, Total	38,000 lbs.	44,000 lbs.	50,000 lbs.	56,000 lbs.	62,000 lbs.	68,000 lbs.	74,000 lbs.	80,000 lbs.
" on Drivers	23,000 "	28,000 "	33,000 "	38,000 "	43,000 "	48,000 "	53,000 "	58,000 "
" on Trucks	15,000 "	16,000 "	17,000 "	18,000 "	19,000 "	20,000 "	21,000 "	22,000 "
Capacity of Tank	400 gal.	450 gal.	500 gal.	625 gal.	700 gal.	800 gal.	900 gal.	1,000 gal.
Hauling Capacity on Level	525 tons.	650 tons.	775 tons	875 tons.	1,000 tons.	1,125 tons.	1,250 tons.	1,875 tons.
" " 20 ft. Grade	255 "	315 "	375 "	425 "	485 "	545 "	605 "	665 "
" " 40 ft. "	170 "	210 "	250 "	285 "	325 "	365 "	405 "	445 "
" " 60 ft. "	125 "	155 "	185 "	210 "	240 "	275 "	300 "	330 "
" " 80 ft. "	100 "	125 "	150 "	170 "	190 "	215 "	240 "	265 "
" " 100 ft. "	85 "	105 "	125 "	140 "	160 "	180 "	200 "	220 "
Prices ready for service at works in Scranton	$	$	$	$	$	$	$	$

DOUBLE-ENDER LOCOMOTIVE.

CLASS J.

The so-called Double-Ender Locomotive, of which particulars are given on the two preceding pages, is designed for switching, suburban, or elevated railroad service, for all of which it is well adapted.

The tank is placed on top of the boiler directly over the driving wheels, which are of small diameter, and there are a leading and a trailing two-wheeled truck, equalized with the adjacent driving wheels, each with a swing bolster and radius bar. The engine has great adhesion in proportion to the total weight, takes curves with ease, runs steadily and equally well in either direction, and does not require turning round. These qualities are eminently suitable for an accelerated service in which rapid preparation, convenience, power, frequent stopping and quick starting are necessary.

On the following page we give the usual general specifications.

GENERAL SPECIFICATIONS.

BOILER.—Made of best cold-blast charcoal plate iron, or all-guaranteed steel plate if required; longitudinal seams double riveted in the larger boilers. Fire box of steel, tubes of best wrought iron set with copper ferrules at both ends; one steam dome fitted with balanced throttle valve; one steam whistle and two safety valves; feed water supplied with one pump and one injector (or two injectors if required); boiler furnished with steam gauge, blow-off cock, gauge cocks and blower valve, and covered with pine lagging and planished iron jacket

CYLINDERS.—Made of close-grained charcoal iron, as hard as can be worked, outside connected, horizontal, bolted together in center, right and left hand interchangeable, heads, sides and steam chest furnished with iron casings.

PISTONS.—Steel rods, cast-iron heads and followers; packing rings of cast iron or brass.

CROSS HEADS—Of charcoal iron or cast steel; guide bars of steel, or case hardened iron, secured to wrought-iron yoke and cylinder head.

CONNECTING RODS.—Best quality hammered iron; boxes of best quality hard brass, lined with babbitt metal.

VALVE MOTION.—Shifting links of hammered iron, case hardened, with all wearing parts bushed and case hardened; rocker shafts and lifting shaft of wrought iron, with solid arms; cast-iron slide valves of the usual pattern.

DRIVING WHEELS.—Cast-iron centers; steel tires; hammered iron or steel axles as required; axle boxes of cast iron with brass bearings; crank pins of steel

TRUCKS.—Swing bolster, with radius bar, equalized with driving wheels; chilled wheels; hammered iron axles; cast-iron axle boxes with brass bearings.

CAB—Of hard wood with plate-glass windows.

PILOTS—Of hard wood or wrought iron.

TANK.—Mounted on top of boiler.

TOOLS.—A complete set of iron and steel wrenches, one screw wrench, two chisels, hard and soft hammers, two jack screws, one pinch bar, and complete set of fire tools and set of oil cans.

MOUNTING, &c.—Running boards and hand rails on each side; one bell and frame; one sand box; brackets and shelf for head light; signal gong; gauge lamp, and all necessary oil cups.

THE "FORNEY" TANK LOCOMOTIVE.

CLASS K.

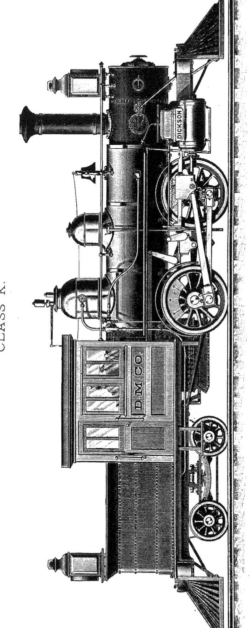

GAUGE, 4 FEET 8½ INCHES.

FUEL, COAL OR WOOD.

The "Forney" Tank Locomotive.

GAUGE, 4 FEET 8½ INCHES.   FUEL, COAL OR WOOD.

DIMENSIONS AND CAPACITIES OF EIGHT SIZES OF THIS CLASS.

CLASS	10—K	11—K	12—K	13—K	14—K	15—K	16—K	17—K
Cylinders, Diameter	10"	11"	12"	13"	14"	15"	16"	17"
" Stroke	16"	16'	18'	20'	20" or 22'	20" or 22'	22" or 24"	22" or 24"
Diameter of Driving Wheels	37½" to 42"	37½" to 42'	40" to 48'	40" to 48'	42" to 50'	44" to 53'	45" to 56'	48' to 58'
" Truck Wheels	24"	24" to 26"	24" to 26'	24" to 26"	24" to 28"	24" to 28'	26" to 30'	26' to 30"
Wheel Base, Rigid	5' 0"	5' 0"	5' 6"	6' 0"	6' 6"	7' 0"	7' 6"	7' 6"
" " Total	16' 3"	16' 6"	17' 9"	18' 6"	19' 9"	20' 7"	21' 8"	22' 6"
Length of Engine without Pilot	26' 9"	27' 7"	29' 2"	30' 1"	31' 7"	32' 10"	34' 4"	35' 3"
" with Pilot	31' 9"	33' 1"	34' 8"	36' 1"	37' 7"	38' 10"	40' 10"	41' 9"
Weight Loaded, Total	39,000 lbs.	45,000 lbs.	51,000 lbs.	57,000 lbs.	63,000 lbs.	70,000 lbs.	77,000 lbs.	84,000 lbs.
" on Drivers	27,000 "	31,000 "	35,000 "	39,000 "	43,000 "	48,000 "	53,000 "	58,000 "
" on Truck	12,000 "	14,000 "	16,000 "	18,000 "	20,000 "	22,000 "	24,000 "	26,000 "
Capacity of Tank	600 gal.	700 gal.	800 gal.	900 gal.	1,000 gal.	1,100 gal.	1,200 gal.	1,300 gal.
Hauling Capacity on Level	675 tons.	775 tons.	875 tons.	975 tons.	1,075 tons.	1,200 tons.	1,325 tons.	1,450 tons.
" 20 ft. Grade	325 "	375 "	425 "	460 "	520 "	560 "	640 "	700 "
" 40 ft. "	220 "	250 "	285 "	315 "	350 "	390 "	430 "	470 "
" 60 ft. "	162 "	185 "	210 "	235 "	260 "	290 "	320 "	350 "
" 80 ft. "	130 "	150 "	165 "	185 "	205 "	230 "	255 "	275 "
" 100 ft. "	105 "	125 "	140 "	155 "	170 "	190 "	210 "	230 "
Prices ready for service at works in Scranton	$	$	$	$	$	$	$	$

THE "FORNEY" TANK LOCOMOTIVE.

CLASS K.

The so-called "Forney" Tank Locomotive is particularly serviceable for suburban traffic, or for switching purposes, either on surface or elevated roads. It runs steadily and rides easily.

General specifications are given on the following page.

GENERAL SPECIFICATIONS.

BOILER.—Made of best cold-blast charcoal plate iron, or all-guaranteed steel plate if required; longitudinal seams of the larger sizes double riveted. Fire box of steel, flues of best wrought iron set with copper ferrules at both ends; one steam dome fitted with balanced throttle valve; one steam whistle and two safety valves; feed water supplied with one pump and one injector (or two injectors if required); boiler furnished with steam gauge, blow-off cock, gauge cocks and blower valve, and covered with pine lagging and planished iron jacket.

CYLINDERS.—Made of close-grained charcoal iron, as hard as can be worked, outside connected, horizontal, bolted together in center, right and left hand interchangeable, heads, sides and steam chest furnished with iron casings.

PISTONS.—Steel rods, cast-iron heads and followers; packing rings of cast iron or brass.

CROSS HEADS—Of charcoal iron or cast steel.

GUIDE BARS—Of steel, or case-hardened iron, secured to wrought iron yoke and cylinder head.

CONNECTING RODS.—Best quality hammered iron; boxes of best quality hard brass, lined with babbitt metal.

VALVE MOTION.—Shifting links of hammered iron, with all wearing parts bushed and case hardened; rocker shafts and lifting shaft of wrought iron, with solid arms; cast-iron slide valves of the usual pattern.

DRIVING WHEELS.—Cast-iron centers; steel tires; hammered iron or steel axles if required; axle boxes, cast iron with brass bearings; crank pins of steel.

CAB—Of hard wood with plate-glass windows.

PILOTS—Of hard wood or wrought iron.

TANK.—Mounted on main frames in rear of boiler; truck wheels double plate, chilled face; hammered iron axles with brass bearings.

TOOLS.—A complete set of iron and steel wrenches, one screw wrench, two chisels, hard and soft hammers, two jack screws, one pinch bar, and complete set of fire tools.

MOUNTING, &c.—Running boards and hand rails on each side; one bell and frame; one sand box; brackets and shelf for head light; signal gong; steam gauge lamp, and all necessary oil cans and oil cups.

DOUBLE-ENDER LOCOMOTIVE.

CLASS L.

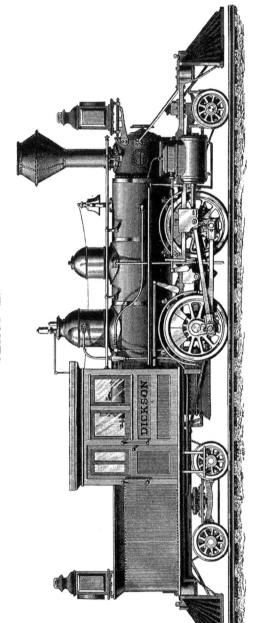

GAUGE, 4 FEET 8½ INCHES.

FUEL, COAL OR WOOD.

DOUBLE-ENDER LOCOMOTIVE.

GAUGE, 4 FEET 8½ INCHES.　　FUEL, COAL OR WOOD.

DIMENSIONS AND CAPACITIES OF EIGHT SIZES OF THIS CLASS.

CLASS	10–L	11–L	12–L	13–L	14–L	15–L.	16–L	17–L
Cylinders, Diameter	10"	11"	12"	13"	14"	15"	16"	17"
" Stroke	16"	16"	18"	20"	20" or 22"	20" or 22"	22" or 24"	22" or 24"
Diameter of Driving Wheels	37½" to 42"	37½" to 42"	40" to 48"	40" to 48"	42" to 50"	44" to 53"	45" to 56"	48" to 56"
" Truck Wheels	24"	24" to 26"	24" to 26"	24" to 26"	24" to 28"	24" to 28"	26" to 30"	26" to 30"
Wheel Base, Rigid	5' 3"	5' 6"	5' 9"	6 ft.	6' 6"	7 ft.	7' 6"	7' 6"
" Total	22' 7"	23' 8"	24' 5"	25' 4"	26' 9"	27' 9"	29' 1"	29' 11"
Length of Engine without Pilots	28' 10"	29' 6"	31' 0"	32' 0"	33' 5"	34' 6"	36' 1"	36' 9"
" with Pilots	33' 10"	35' 0"	36' 6"	38' 0"	39' 5"	40' 6"	42' 7"	43' 3"
Weight, Loaded, Total	42,000 lbs.	48,000 lbs.	54,000 lbs.	60,000 lbs.	67,000 lbs.	74,000 lbs.	81,000 lbs.	88,000 lbs.
" on Drivers	24,000 "	27,000 "	30,000 "	33,000 "	37,000 "	41,000 "	45,000 "	49,000 "
" on Trucks	18,000 "	21,000 "	24,000 "	27,000 "	30,000 "	33,000 "	36,000 "	39,000 "
Capacity of Tank	600 gal.	700 gal.	800 gal.	900 gal.	1,000 gal.	1,100 gal.	1,200 gal.	1,300 gal.
Hauling Capacity on Level	550 tons.	625 tons.	700 tons.	750 tons.	850 tons.	950 tons.	1,050 tons.	1,150 tons.
" 20 ft. Grade	265	305	340	365	410	460	510	560
" 40 ft. "	180	205	230	245	275	310	345	375
" 60 ft. "	135	150	170	180	205	230	255	275
" 80 ft. "	95	120	135	145	165	180	200	220
" 100 ft. "	90	100	110	120	135	150	165	185

Prices ready for service at works in Scranton........

Double-Ender Locomotive.

CLASS L.

The " Double-Ender " Locomotive is a type of engine well adapted to suburban service, or switching, and is suitable for elevated as well as surface roads.

The tank is placed over the rear truck, and the variation in the quantity of fuel and water in service affects the adhesion of the driving wheels but slightly. The leading truck has a swing bolster and radius bar allowing the engine to curve freely. The engine has great adhesion in proportion to its total weight, runs steadily and equally well in either direction, and does not require turning round. These qualities are highly important in an accelerated service in which rapid preparation, convenience, power, frequent stopping and quick starting are necessary.

On the following page we give the usual specifications.

GENERAL SPECIFICATIONS.

BOILER.—Made of best cold-blast charcoal plate iron, or all-guaranteed steel plate if required; longitudinal seams of the larger sizes double riveted. Fire box of steel, flues of best wrought iron set with copper ferrules at both ends; one steam dome fitted with balanced throttle valve; one steam whistle and two safety valves; feed water supplied with one pump and one injector (or two injectors if required); boiler furnished with steam gauge, blow-off cock, gauge cocks and blower valve, and covered with pine lagging and planished iron jacket.

CYLINDERS.—Made of close-grained charcoal iron, as hard as can be worked, outside connected, horizontal, bolted together in center, right and left hand interchangeable, heads, sides and steam chest furnished with iron casings.

PISTONS.—Steel rods, cast-iron heads and followers; packing rings of cast iron or brass.

CROSS HEADS—Of charcoal iron or cast steel.

GUIDE BARS—Of steel, or case-hardened iron, secured to wrought-iron yoke and cylinder head.

CONNECTING RODS.—Best quality hammered iron; boxes of best quality hard brass, lined with babbitt metal.

VALVE MOTION.—Shifting links of hammered iron, case hardened, with all wearing parts bushed and case hardened; rocker shafts and lifting shaft of wrought iron, with solid arms; cast-iron slide valves of the usual pattern.

DRIVING WHEELS.—Cast-iron centers; steel tires; hammered iron or steel axles, if required; axle boxes of cast iron with brass bearings; crank pins of steel.

ENGINE TRUCK.—Swing bolster, with chilled wheels; hammered iron axles; cast-iron axle boxes with brass bearings.

CAB—Of hard wood with plate-glass windows.

PILOT—Of hard wood or wrought iron.

TANK.—Mounted on main frames in rear of boiler; truck wheels double plate, chilled face; hammered iron axles with brass bearings.

TOOLS.—A complete set of iron and steel wrenches, one screw wrench, two chisels, hard and soft hammers, two jack screws, one pinch bar, and complete set of fire tools.

MOUNTING, &c.—Running boards and hand rails on each side; one bell and frame; one sand box; brackets and shelf for head light; signal gong; steam gauge lamp, and all necessary oil cans and oil cups.

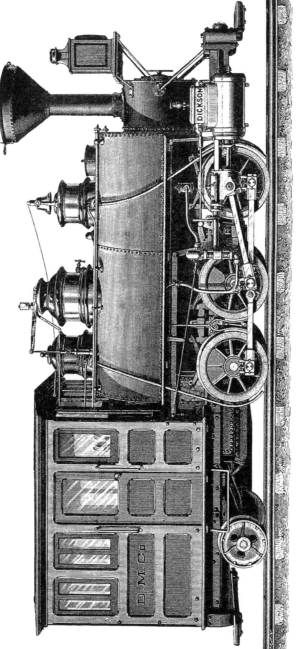

SIX WHEELS COUPLED TANK SWITCHING LOCOMOTIVE.

WITH TRAILING TRUCK.

CLASS M.

GAUGE, 4 FEET 8½ INCHES.

FUEL, COAL OR WOOD.

CHICAGO, FAIRCHILD & EAU CLAIR RIVER No. 3 – Dickson No. 449 – 1883

SIX WHEELS COUPLED TANK SWITCHING LOCOMOTIVE—WITH TRAILING TRUCK.

GAUGE, 4 FEET 8½ INCHES.   FUEL, COAL OR WOOD.

DIMENSIONS AND CAPACITIES OF SIX SIZES OF THIS CLASS.

CLASS	14—M	15—M	16—M	17—M	18—M	19—M
Cylinders, Diameter	14″	15″	16″	17″	18″	19′
" Stroke	22″	22″	22″ or 24″	22″ or 24″	22″ or 24″	22″ or 24″
Diameter of Driving Wheels	40″ to 50″	42″ to 54″	42″ to 54″	42″ to 54″	44″ to 56″	44″ to 56″
" Truck Wheels	26″ to 30″	26″ to 30″	26″ to 30″	26″ to 30″	28″ to 30″	28″ to 30″
Wheel Base, Rigid	9′ 9″	10′ 0″	10′ 0″	10′ 3″	10′ 6″	10′ 9″
" " Total	18′ 3″	18′ 9″	19′ 3″	19′ 9″	20′ 6″	21′ 0″
Length of Engine without Pilots	30′ 3″	31′ 0″	32′ 0″	32′ 9″	34′ 0″	34′ 6″
" with One Pilot	33′ 3″	34′ 3″	35′ 3″	36′ 3″	37′ 6″	38′ 0″
Weight, Loaded, Total	69,000 lbs.	75,000 lbs.	81,000 lbs.	87,000 lbs.	93,000 lbs.	99,000 lbs.
" on Drivers	56,000 "	62,000 "	67,000 "	73,000 "	78,000 "	84,000 "
" on Truck	18,000 "	13,000 "	14,000 "	14,000 "	15,000 "	15,600 "
Capacity of Tank	800 gal.	850 gal.	900 gal.	930 gal.	1,000 gal.	1,050 gal.
Hauling Capacity on Level	1,350 tons.	1,475 tons.	1,625 tons.	1,750 tons.	1,875 tons.	2,000 tons.
" " 20 ft. Grade	650 "	710 "	785 "	845 "	905 "	965 "
" " " 40 ft. "	435 "	475 "	525 "	585 "	605 "	645 "
" " " 60 ft. "	320 "	350 "	390 "	420 "	450 "	480 "
" " " 80 ft. "	255 "	280 "	310 "	330 "	355 "	380 "
" " " 100 ft. "	210 "	230 "	255 "	275 "	295 "	315 "
Prices ready for service at works in Scranton						

TANK SWITCHING ENGINE.

CLASS M.

We give particulars of several sizes of this class of Switching Engine, which has six wheels coupled and a trailing two-wheeled truck. The tank is placed either over the boiler, as shown in the engraving, or over the truck.

The locomotive is designed for switching about depots and stations, or for logging or plantation service. The rear truck, which is used whether the tank is on the boiler or not, is of the swing-bolster, radius-bar kind, and permits the engine to pass around curves with safety, and increases its steadiness.

General specifications are given on the next page.

GENERAL SPECIFICATIONS.

BOILER.—Made of best cold-blast charcoal plate iron, or all-guaranteed steel plate if required; longitudinal seams double riveted for the larger sizes. Fire box of steel, tubes of best wrought iron set with copper ferrules at both ends; one steam dome fitted with balanced throttle valve; one steam whistle and two safety valves; feed water supplied with one pump and one injector (or two injectors if required); boiler furnished with steam gauge, blow-off cock, gauge cocks and blower valve, and covered with pine lagging and planished iron jacket.

CYLINDERS.—Made of close-grained charcoal iron, as hard as can be worked, outside connected, horizontal, bolted together in center, right and left hand interchangeable, heads, sides and steam chest furnished with iron casings.

PISTONS.—Steel rods, cast-iron heads and followers; packing rings of cast iron or brass.

CROSS HEADS—of charcoal iron or cast steel.

GUIDE BARS—Of steel, or case-hardened iron, secured to wrought-iron yoke and cylinder head.

CONNECTING RODS.—Best quality hammered iron; boxes of best quality hard brass lined with babbitt metal.

VALVE MOTION.—Shifting links of hammered iron, case hardened, with all wearing parts bushed and case hardened; rocker shafts and lifting shaft of wrought iron, with solid arms; cast-iron slide valves of the usual pattern.

DRIVING WHEELS.—Cast-iron centers; steel tires; hammered iron or steel axles as required; axle boxes, cast iron with brass bearings; crank pins of steel.

TRUCK.—Swing bolster, with radius bar; chilled wheels; hammered iron axles; cast-iron axle boxes with brass bearings.

CAB—Of hard wood with plate-glass windows.

PILOT—Of hard wood or wrought iron.

TANK.—Mounted on top of boiler or over truck.

TOOLS.—A complete set of iron and steel wrenches, one screw wrench, two chisels, hard and soft hammers, two jack screws, one pinch bar, and complete set of fire tools and set of oil cans.

MOUNTING, &c.—Running boards and hand rails on each side; one bell and frame; one sand box; brackets and shelf for head light; signal gong; gauge lamp, and all necessary oil cups.

Tank Switching Engine.

CLASS N.

WITH LEADING AND TRAILING TRUCKS.

The Class "N" locomotive differs from Class "M" only in the addition of a leading two-wheeled truck, which has the effect to steady the engine when running forward, and does away with the necessity for turning the engine around.

We add a table of hauling capacities for this class, but the specifications are similar to those of Class "M."

Six Wheels Coupled Tank Switching Engine—With Leading and Trailing Two-Wheeled Trucks.

GAUGE, 4 FEET 8½ INCHES.   FUEL, COAL OR WOOD.

DIMENSIONS AND CAPACITIES OF SIX SIZES OF THIS CLASS.

CLASS	14—N	15—N	16—N	17—N	18—N	19—N
Cylinders, Diameter	14″	15″	16″	17″	18″	19″
" Stroke	22″	22″	22″ or 24″	22″ or 24	22″ or 24″	22″ or 24″
Diameter of Driving Wheels	40″ to 50″	42″ to 54″	42″ to 54″	42″ to 54″	44″ to 56″	44″ to 56″
" Truck Wheels	26″ to 30″	26″ to 30″	26″ to 30″	26″ to 30″	28″ to 30″	28″ to 30″
Wheel Base, Rigid	9′ 9″	10′ 0″	10′ 0″	10′ 3″	10′ 6″	10′ 9″
" " Total	22′ 6″	23′ 3″	23′ 9″	24′ 3″	25′ 4″	26′ 1″
Length of Engine without Pilots	28′ 6″	29′ 3″	30′ 0″	30′ 9″	31′ 6″	32′ 3″
" with Two Pilots	34′ 6″	35′ 9″	36′ 6″	37′ 9″	38′ 6″	39′ 3″
Weight, Loaded, Total	72,000 lbs.	78,000 lbs.	84,000 lbs.	90,000 lbs.	96,000 lbs.	102,000 lbs.
" on Drivers	53,000 "	58,000 "	63,000 "	68,000 "	78,000 "	78,000 "
" on Trucks	19,000 "	20,000 "	21,000 "	22,000 "	23,000 "	24,000 "
Capacity of Tank	800 gal.	850 gal.	900 gal.	950 gal.	1,000 gal.	1,050 gal.
Hauling Capacity on Level	1,250 tons.	1,375 tons.	1,500 tons.	1,600 tons.	1,725 tons.	1,850 tons.
" " 20 ft. Grade	605 "	665 "	725 "	770 "	830 "	895 "
" " 40 ft. "	405 "	445 "	485 "	515 "	555 "	595 "
" " 60 ft. "	300 "	330 "	360 "	380 "	410 "	440 "
" " 80 ft. "	235 "	260 "	285 "	305 "	325 "	350 "
" " 100 ft. "	195 "	215 "	235 "	250 "	270 "	290 "
Prices ready for service at works in Scranton	$$	$$	$$	$$	$$	$$

Six Wheels Coupled "Forney" Tank Locomotive.

Class O.

Gauge, 4 Feet 8½ Inches.

Fuel, Coal or Wood.

SIX WHEELS COUPLED "FORNEY" TANK LOCOMOTIVE.

GAUGE, 4 FEET 8½ INCHES.   FUEL, COAL OR WOOD.

DIMENSIONS AND CAPACITIES OF SIX SIZES OF THIS CLASS.

CLASS	14—O	15—O	16—O	17—O	18—O	19—O
Cylinders, Diameter	14"	15"	16"	17"	18"	19"
" Stroke	22"	22"	22" or 24"	22" or 24"	22" or 24"	22" or 24"
Diameter of Driving Wheels	40" to 50"	42" to 54"	42" to 54"	42" to 54"	44" to 56"	41" to 56"
" Truck Wheels	26" to 30"	26" to 30"	26" to 30"	26" to 30"	28" to 30"	28" to 30"
Wheel Base, Rigid	9' 9"	10' 0"	10' 0"	10' 3"	10' 6"	10' 9"
" " Total	20' 9"	21' 3"	21' 9"	22' 6"	23' 0"	23' 6"
Length of Engine without Pilot	32' 9"	33' 9"	34' 9"	35' 6"	36' 3"	37' 0"
" " with one Pilot	35' 9"	37' 0"	38' 0"	38' 9"	39' 9"	40' 6"
Weight, Loaded, Total	74,000 lbs.	80,000 lbs.	86,000 lbs.	92,000 lbs.	98,000 lbs.	104,000 lbs.
" " on Drivers	54,000 "	58,000 "	62,000 "	66,000 "	72,000 "	77,000 "
" " on Truck	20,000 "	22,000 "	24,000 "	26,000 "	26,000 "	27,000 "
Capacity of Tank	1,000 gal.	1,100 gal.	1,200 gal.	1,300 gal.	1,400 gal.	1,500 gal.
Hauling Capacity on Level	1,800 tons.	1,400 tons.	1,500 tons.	1,625 tons.	1,750 tons.	1,900 tons.
" 20 ft. Grade	625 "	675 "	725 "	785 "	845 "	920 "
" 40 ft. "	420 "	450 "	485 "	525 "	565 "	615 "
" 60 ft. "	310 "	335 "	360 "	390 "	420 "	455 "
" 80 ft. "	245 "	265 "	285 "	310 "	330 "	360 "
" 100 ft. "	205 "	220 "	235 "	255 "	275 "	300 "
Prices ready for service at works in Scranton	$	$	$	$	$	$

Six Wheels Coupled "Forney" Tank Locomotive.

CLASS O.

The Class "O" locomotive is a very powerful type of engine for its weight, and is designed for service where frequent stops are necessary with heavy loads, and therefore where it will be possible to take water often. The tank is made small in order to keep down the dead weight of the engine and to shorten the wheel base. Although this engine is intended to be run in either direction, and is often so used, it will be found to "track" better and to diminish the wear of flanges if it is run backwards. It, however, runs steadily at all times, and is perfectly free from plunging. The position of the cab renders the engine remarkably easy riding.

The driving wheels are all equalized together, thus giving great vertical flexibility of wheel base. The truck is center bearing, and provided with a swing bolster.

We add general specifications.

GENERAL SPECIFICATIONS.

BOILER.—Made of best cold-blast charcoal plate iron, or all-guaranteed steel plate if required; longitudinal seams of the larger boilers double riveted. Fire box of steel, flues of best wrought iron set with copper ferrules at both ends; one steam dome fitted with balanced throttle valve; one steam whistle and two safety valves; feed water supplied with one pump and one injector (or two injectors if required); boiler furnished with steam gauge, blow-off cock, gauge cocks and blower valve, and covered with pine lagging and planished iron jacket.

CYLINDERS.—Made of close-grained charcoal iron, as hard as can be worked, outside connected, horizontal, bolted together in center, right and left hand interchangeable, heads, sides and steam chest furnished with iron casings.

PISTONS.—Steel rods, cast-iron heads and followers; packing rings of cast iron or brass.

CROSS HEADS—Of charcoal iron or cast steel.

GUIDE BARS—Of steel, or case-hardened iron, secured to wrought-iron yoke and cylinder head.

CONNECTING RODS.—Best quality hammered iron; boxes of best quality hard brass, lined with babbitt metal.

VALVE MOTION.—Shifting links of hammered iron, with all wearing parts bushed and case hardened; rocker shafts and lifting shaft of wrought iron, with solid arms; cast-iron slide valves of the usual pattern.

DRIVING WHEELS.—Cast-iron centers; steel tires; hammered iron or steel axles if required; axle boxes of cast iron with brass bearings; crank pins of steel.

CAB—Of hard wood with plate-glass windows.

PILOTS—Of hard wood or wrought iron.

TANK.—Mounted on main frames in rear of boiler; truck wheels double plate, chilled face; hammered iron axles with brass bearings.

TOOLS.—A complete set of iron and steel wrenches, one screw wrench, two chisels, hard and soft hammers, two jack screws, one pinch bar, and complete set of fire tools.

MOUNTING, &c.—Running boards and hand rails on each side; one bell and frame; one sand box; brackets and shelf for head light; signal gong; steam gauge lamp, and all necessary oil cans and oil cups.

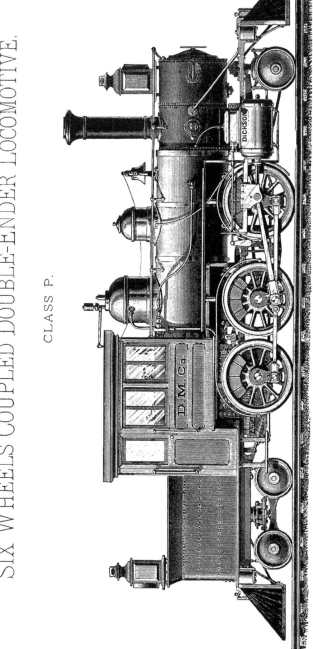

SIX WHEELS COUPLED DOUBLE-ENDER LOCOMOTIVE.

CLASS P.

GAUGE, 4 FEET 8½ INCHES.

FUEL, COAL OR WOOD.

SIX WHEELS COUPLED DOUBLE-ENDER LOCOMOTIVE.

GAUGE, 4 FEET 8½ INCHES.　　FUEL, COAL OR WOOD.

DIMENSIONS AND CAPACITIES OF SIX SIZES OF THIS CLASS.

CLASS	14–P	15–P	16–P	17–P	18–P	19–P
Cylinders, Diameter	14″	15″	16″	17″	18″	19″
" Stroke	22″	22″	22″ or 24″	22″ or 24″	22″ or 24″	22″ or 24″
Diameter of Driving Wheels	40″ to 50″	42″ to 54″	42″ to 54″	42″ to 54″	44″ to 56″	44″ to 56″
" Truck Wheels	26″ to 30″	26″ to 30″	26″ to 30″	26″ to 30″	28″ to 30″	28″ to 30″
Wheel Base, Rigid	9′ 9″	10′ 0″	10′ 0″	10′ 3″	10′ 6″	10′ 9″
" " Total	27′ 10″	28′ 6″	29′ 3″	30′ 0″	30′ 9″	31′ 6″
Length of Engine without Pilot	34′ 9″	35′ 6″	36′ 3″	37′ 3″	38′ 0″	38′ 9″
" with one Pilot	37′ 9″	38′ 9″	39′ 6″	40′ 6″	41′ 6″	42′ 3″
Weight Loaded, Total	78,000 lbs.	84,000 lbs.	90,000 lbs.	96,000 lbs.	102,000 lbs.	108,000 lbs.
" on Drivers	52,000 "	56,000 "	60,000 "	64,000 "	69,000 "	74,000 "
" on Truck	26,000 "	28,000 "	30,000 "	32,000 "	33,000 "	34,000 "
Capacity of Tank	1,000 gal.	1,100 gal.	1,200 gal.	1,300 gal.	1,400 gal.	1,500 gal.
Hauling Capacity on Level	1,250 tons.	1,375 tons.	1,500 tons	1,600 tons.	1,725 tons.	1,850 tons.
" 20 ft. Grade	605 "	665 "	725 "	770 "	830 "	895 "
" 40 ft. "	405 "	445 "	485 "	515 "	555 "	595 "
" 60 ft. "	300 "	330 "	360 "	380 "	410 "	440 "
" 80 ft. "	235 "	260 "	285 "	305 "	325 "	350 "
" 100 ft. "	195 "	215 "	235 "	250 "	270 "	290 "
Prices ready for service at works in Scranton	$	$	$	$	$	$

Six Wheels Coupled Double-Ender Locomotive.

CLASS P.

The Class "P" locomotive is offered as an excellent type of engine to conduct any heavy traffic in which stops and opportunities to take water are frequent. The tank is placed over the rear truck, and is made small in order to keep down the dead weight and to shorten the wheel base. It will be found to track well in either direction, and will not require turning around.

The pony truck is provided with a swing bolster and radius bar, and is equalized with the front pair of driving wheels, the latter being equalized with each other. This arrangement gives great vertical flexibility to the wheel base, and the engine will ride smoothly over the poorest tracks. The rear truck is, like the pony truck, provided with a swing bolster. The engine is remarkably comfortable to the engine men, from the position of the cab; and for branch freight or mixed service, or, as indicated above, for any service where there are short runs and frequent stops, necessitating power and quick starting, the performance will be in every way satisfactory.

Specifications follow.

GENERAL SPECIFICATIONS.

BOILER.—Made of best cold-blast charcoal plate iron, or all-guaranteed steel plate if required; longitudinal seams double riveted. Fire box of steel, flues of best wrought iron set with copper ferrules at both ends; one steam dome fitted with balanced throttle valve; one steam whistle and two safety valves; feed water supplied with one pump and one injector (or two injectors if required); boiler furnished with steam gauge, blow-off cock, gauge cocks and blower valve, and covered with pine lagging and planished iron jacket.

CYLINDERS.—Made of close-grained charcoal iron, as hard as can be worked, outside connected, horizontal, bolted together in center, right and left hand interchangeable, heads, sides and steam chest furnished with iron casings.

PISTONS.—Steel rods, cast-iron heads and followers; packing rings of cast iron or brass.

CROSS HEADS—Of charcoal iron or cast steel.

GUIDE BARS—Of steel, or case-hardened iron, secured to wrought-iron yoke and cylinder head.

CONNECTING RODS.—Best quality hammered iron; boxes of best quality hard brass, lined with babbitt metal.

VALVE MOTION.—Shifting links of hammered iron, case hardened, with all wearing parts bushed and case hardened; rocker shafts and lifting shaft of wrought iron, with solid arms; cast-iron slide valves of the usual pattern.

DRIVING WHEELS.—Cast-iron centers; steel tires; hammered iron or steel axles, as preferred; axle boxes of cast iron with brass bearings; crank pins of steel.

ENGINE TRUCK.—Swing bolster, with chilled wheels; hammered iron axles; cast-iron axle boxes with brass bearings.

CAB—Of hard wood with plate-glass windows.

PILOTS—Of hard wood or wrought iron.

TANK.—Mounted on main frames in rear of boiler; truck wheels double plate, chilled face; hammered iron axles with brass bearings.

TOOLS.—A complete set of iron and steel wrenches, one screw wrench, two chisels, hard and soft hammers, two jack screws, one pinch bar, and complete set of fire tools.

MOUNTING, &c.—Running boards and hand rails on each side; one bell and frame; one sand box; brackets and shelf for head light; signal gong; steam gauge lamp, and all necessary oil cans and oil cups,

Hydraulic Flanging.

By the treatment which a plate receives when flanged by hand, the edge is alternately elongated and compressed, and subjected to damaging extremes of temperature : neither is it free from liability to burn. Moreover, at the completion of the operation it is far from being flat and uniformly curved, and requires considerable working to fit it in its place.

The advantages of hydraulic flanging, apart from its rapidity *per se*, are that the plate is heated in a special furnace to a moderate, uniform temperature throughout, the flanging is all done at one operation in two or three minutes' time, so that the metal flows into its new form with but little strain, and the plate is left flat and exact in shape.

ROUND HEADS.

THE DICKSON MFG. CO. keep in stock, and can supply immediately upon the receipt of orders, round boiler heads of the sizes given in the table below, and at prices which are but a small advance upon the cost of the plain sheet. These heads are made of plates furnished by the Nashua Iron and Steel Co., Nashua, N. H., and are guaranteed to have a tensile strength of 60,000 lbs. per square inch, and an elastic limit of 33,000 lbs. per square inch.

We can offer Round Heads :—

From 20 inches to 26 inches in diameter, inclusive, at_____per lb.
From 28 inches to 48 inches, inclusive, ... at_____per lb.
From 50 inches to 72 inches, inclusive, ... at_____per lb.

Prices subject to change without notice.

DIMENSIONS OF ROUND HEADS,
With a flange 2½ inches high.

Outside diameter, inches	20	22	24	26	28	30	32	34	36	38	40	42	44	46	48	50	52	54	56	58	60	62	64	66	68	70	72
Thickness of plate	$\frac{3}{8}$	$\frac{3}{8}$	$\frac{3}{8}$	$\frac{13}{32}$	$\frac{13}{32}$	$\frac{13}{32}$	$\frac{7}{16}$	$\frac{7}{16}$	$\frac{7}{16}$	$\frac{7}{16}$	$\frac{7}{16}$	$\frac{7}{16}$	$\frac{7}{16}$	$\frac{7}{16}$	$\frac{7}{16}$	$\frac{1}{2}$	$\frac{1}{2}$	$\frac{1}{2}$	$\frac{1}{2}$	$\frac{1}{2}$	$\frac{17}{32}$	$\frac{17}{32}$	$\frac{9}{16}$	$\frac{9}{16}$	$\frac{9}{16}$	$\frac{9}{16}$	$\frac{9}{16}$

For sizes larger than 72 inches in diameter, we will make special prices.

BACK HEAD AND TUBE SHEETS
FOR LOCOMOTIVE BOILERS.

We have a large stock of formers for locomotive boiler work, and can offer back heads and flue sheets of such sizes as we have, much cheaper than they can be flanged by hand, and much better. For special shapes and sizes, if ordered in quantities, we will make special prices.

On the following pages we give engravings of some of the back heads and tube sheets for which we have formers.

BACK HEAD SHEETS FOR LOCOMOTIVES

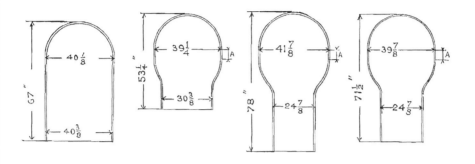

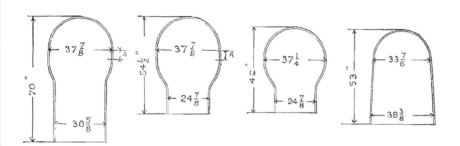

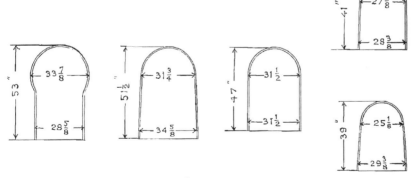

The dimension marked "A", and also the total height of heads, can be varied to any extent desired.

BACK HEAD SHEETS FOR LOCOMOTIVES

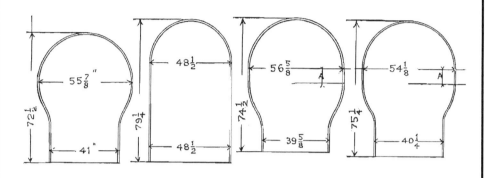

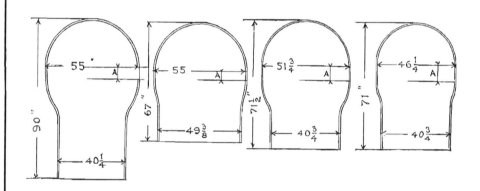

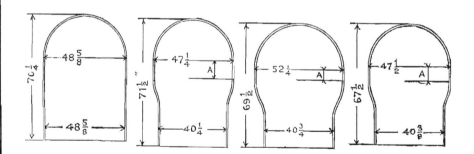

The dimension marked "A", and also the total height of heads, can be varied to any extent desired.

BACK HEAD SHEETS FOR LOCOMOTIVES

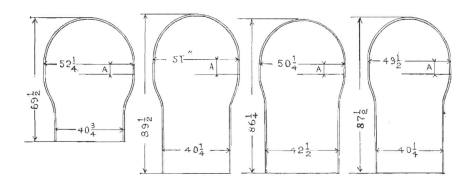

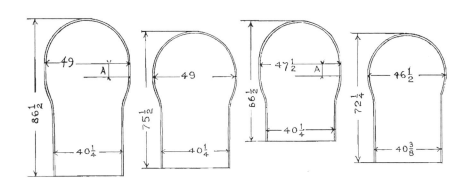

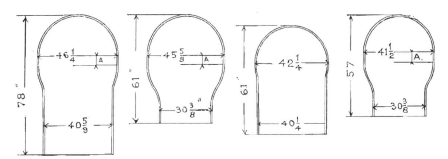

The dimension marked "A", and also the total height of heads, can be varied to any extent desired

Back Flue Head sheets for Locomotives

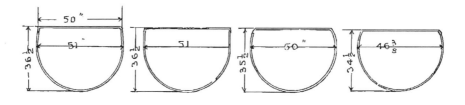

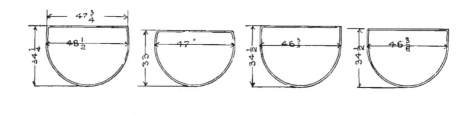

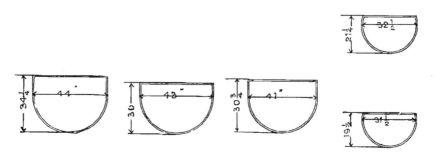

FIRE BOX END SHEETS FOR LOCOMOTIVES

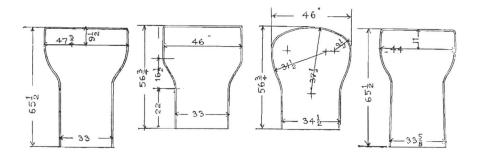

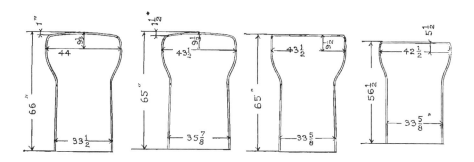

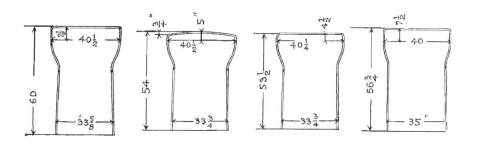

The width and length of these sheets can be varied to any extent desired.

Fire Box end sheets for Locomotives

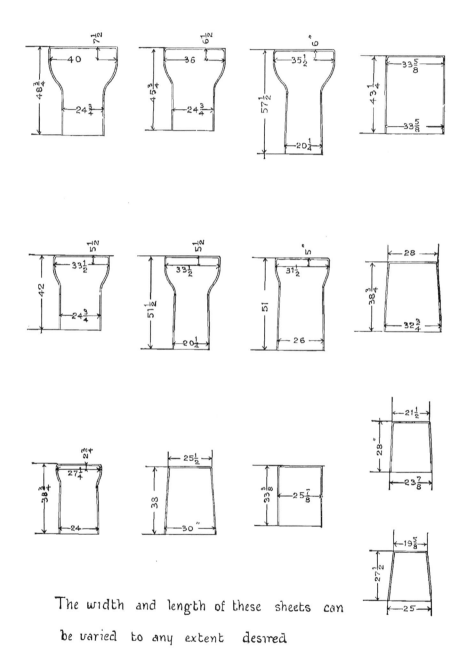

The width and length of these sheets can be varied to any extent desired

LOCOMOTIVE TANKS.

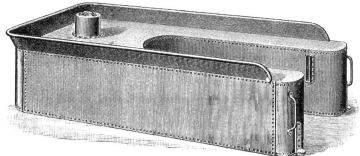

FIG. 1.

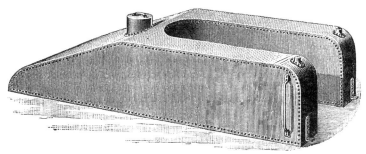

FIG. 2.

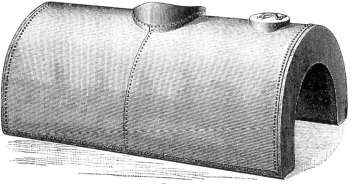

FIG. 3.

THE DICKSON MFG. CO. is prepared to take contracts to build locomotive tanks for railroad companies and others. Some of the usual designs are shown in the cuts above. FIG. 1 shows a tank for separate tenders. FIG. 2 a special form for separate tenders of switching engines, the slope of the top permitting the engine men to see close to the rear of the tender. FIG. 3 shows the best form of saddle tank to use on top of the boiler.

These tanks are made of the best tank iron or steel, and the workmanship is first class throughout.

Prices upon application.

Locomotive Castings and Forgings.

THE DICKSON MANUFACTURING CO. are prepared to make for railroad companies and others, all castings and forgings used in locomotive construction and about railroads generally. A number of these are illustrated on the following pages, and will be made of any desired material and furnished either rough, rough finished or finished to dimensions.

Wheels will be furnished on axles if desired.

CYLINDER.

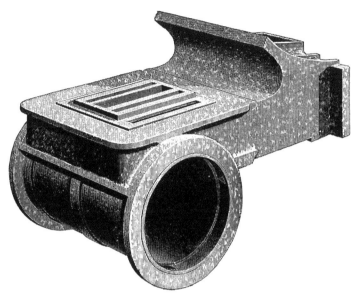

FIG. 4.

These cylinders are made of the best close-grained iron as hard as can be worked. The castings are sound and smooth. They are made reversible and interchangeable.

PRICES OF CYLINDERS.

Diameter in Inches.	Stroke in Inches.	Rough, Per lb.	Bored.	Bored and Planed.	Finished Complete.

DRIVING WHEEL.

FIG. 5.

Driving wheels are made of good, strong close-grained iron. The counterweights are cast in, unless otherwise ordered; the rim and arms are solid or cast hollow, as preferred. The rim and counterweights are divided in several places to diminish the inherent strains due to cooling.

PRICES OF DRIVING WHEELS.

Diameter of Casting.	Rough, Per lb.	Finished, Per lb.

Special prices will be given for fitting wheels with axles and tires.

Engine Truck Wheel.

FIG. 6.

FIG. 6 represents a truck wheel made to receive a steel tire.   They are made of the best quality of iron.

PRICES OF TRUCK WHEELS, TO RECEIVE STEEL TIRES.

Diameter of Centre.	Centre Rough, Per lb.	Centre Finished, Per lb.	Finished Wheel with Tire 2½" thick, Each.	Pair of Finished Wheels with Tires, fitted on Axles.
20"				
23½"				
25"				
26"				

CHILLED PLATE AND SPOKE WHEELS.

At the Wilkes-Barre Works THE DICKSON MANUFACTURING CO. make a specialty of chilled-face, double-plate wheels for locomotive trucks, tenders, and for cars. The wheels are warranted to be sound, smooth on the tread, evenly chilled, truly circular, and will be paired so as to have the wheels on one axle of the same diameter.

PRICES OF CHILLED WHEELS.

Diameter on Tread, in Inches.	Price of Plate Wheel, Rough	Price of Plate Wheel, Bored and Faced.	Price of Spoke Wheel, Rough.	Price of Spoke Wheel, Bored and Faced.	Price of a Pair Wheels fitted on a Finished Axle.
20					
22					
24					
26					
28					
30					
33					

CROSS HEADS.

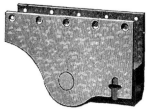

FIG. 7.

These cross heads are made of wrought iron, cast steel, or charcoal iron.

PRICES OF CROSS HEADS, PER POUND.

	Rough.	Finished.
Wrought Iron,		
Cast Steel,		
Charcoal Iron,		

The Steel-Tire Spring-Plate Car Wheel.

(H. M. BOIES PATENT, DECEMBER 18, 1883.)

FIG. 8.

The construction of this wheel is such that the rolled steel tire is joined to the cast hub by two curved steel plates of such shapes as to oppose an elastic resistance in every direction from which strains and blows affect it. The great tensile strength and elasticity of the metal in these plates permits complete security from their breaking to coincide with the least dead weight in parts not exposed to wear, and the vibrations excited by the constant pounding of the tread of the wheel on the rail are lost in the spring of the curves before they reach the axle, so that this active cause of crystallization of axles is largely removed.

The expansion and contraction of the tire from heat induced by the application of the brakes and subsequent cooling, is permitted to occur by the curved shape of the plates without impairing the strength or durability of the wheel.

The shape of the plates between the bolts forms a *hollow spoke* between hub and tire, giving a maximum of strength for the amount of metal used.

The tire is firmly bolted to the plates through a heavy internal flange, which renders it impossible for it to get off the wheel by accident, and not only avoids the weakening of the tire by grooves, slots or holes, but actually reinforces it to such an extent that it can be worn or turned down to its extreme limit of service, and in case it should break the parts would still be held firmly in place by the bolts.

The outer flanges of the plates constitute a supporting arch inside the tire as elastic as the tire itself, and also contributes to the durability of the tire.

The inner or central flanges of the plates are shrunken on each end of the hub supporting the weight, and are also steel bands strengthening and binding the hub to the axle, so that the wheel would run if the hub should be burst or broken.

The thrust of the axle is expended upon an arched spring of a strong curve in the opposite plate.

This wheel is composed of *only four principal parts*, the tire, two plates and the hub, which is less than are found in any other steel-tired wheel that we know of.

The tires are rolled from the best open-hearth or crucible steel, and are matched in pairs of the same metal, so as to wear equally, and when worn out can be quickly and easily replaced in any properly equipped shop.

The plates are of the best open-hearth steel, formed hot by hydraulic pressure and annealed.

The bolts are of the best iron, accurately fitted into reamed holes, and the hubs of strong cast iron.

The parts are put together in the very best manner to insure durability.

This wheel is not weakened by the heat engendered by the application of the brakes.

Its elasticity prevents deterioration from the constant pounding on the rail.

It will not absorb moisture and burst or break from frost.

It is not subject to the breakages to which cast iron is liable.

It reduces the danger of accidents caused by the breaking of axles.

It is considerably lighter than other steel-tired wheels, and thus diminishes the constant traction load.

We believe it is the best, as well as the cheapest, steel-tired wheel in the market.

It has been successfully tested since June, 1884, by constant use in the passenger-car service on the Delaware & Hudson Canal Company Railroad, on the Pennsylvania Division.

We are prepared to supply these wheels promptly, either 33 inches or 42 inches in diameter, in pairs, on the master car-builder's axle, of the best hammered iron from No. 1 wrought scrap, without charge for mounting, or bored to gauge as may be desired, and guarantee the wheels against breakage in ordinary use as long as the tires last.

PRICES.

33-in. wheel, 2¼-in. tire, master car-builder's tread and flange, $ each.

42-in. wheel, 2¼-in. tire, master car-builder's tread and flange,   each.

Axles, master car-builder's standard,   cents per pound.

AXLES.

DRIVING AXLE.

DRIVING AXLE.

DRIVING AXLE.

ENGINE TRUCK AXLE.

TENDER OR CAR TRUCK AXLE.

FIG. 9.

These axles are made of the best hammered iron, or of forged open-hearth steel, and will be furnished rough, rough finished or finished to dimensions.

PRICES OF AXLES, PER POUND.

Kind of Axle.	Iron, Forging.	Iron, Rough Turned.	Iron, Finished.	Steel, Forging.	Steel, Rough Turned.	Steel, Finished.
Driving, with reduced middle,						
Driving, uniform diameter,						
Driving Crank,						
Engine Truck,						
Engine Tender,						
Car,						

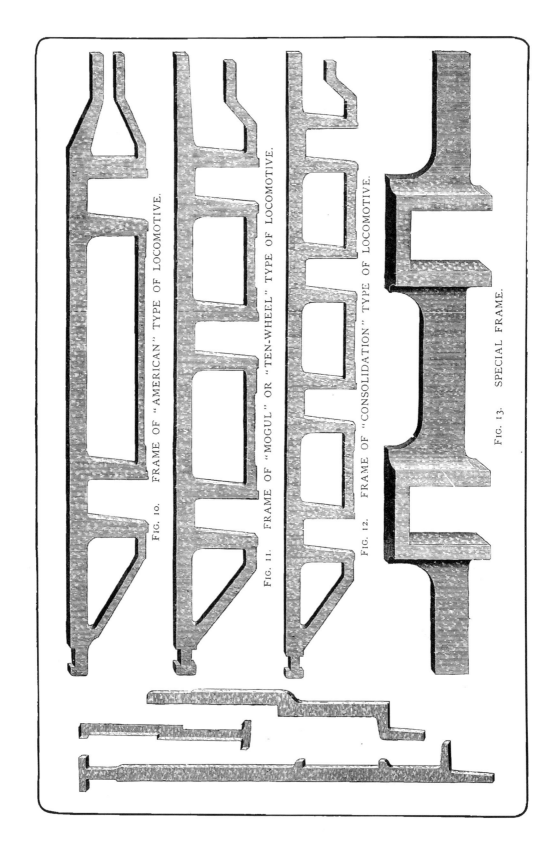

FIG. 10. FRAME OF "AMERICAN" TYPE OF LOCOMOTIVE.

FIG. 11. FRAME OF "MOGUL" OR "TEN-WHEEL" TYPE OF LOCOMOTIVE.

FIG. 12. FRAME OF "CONSOLIDATION" TYPE OF LOCOMOTIVE.

FIG. 13. SPECIAL FRAME.

These frames are made of the best hammered iron, and are either forged solid as shown in the engravings, or built up, and will be furnished in the rough, planed or planed and fitted.

PRICE LIST OF FRAMES, PER POUND.

DESIGNATION.	Forged.	Planed.	Planed and Slotted.	Drilled and Fitted.
"American," solid,				
"American," built up,				
"Mogul," solid,				
"Mogul," built up,				
"Ten Wheel," solid,				
"Ten-Wheel," built up,				
"Consolidation," solid,				
"Consolidation," built up.				
Special,				

CONNECTING RODS.

FIG. 14.

FIG. 15.

Coupling Rods.

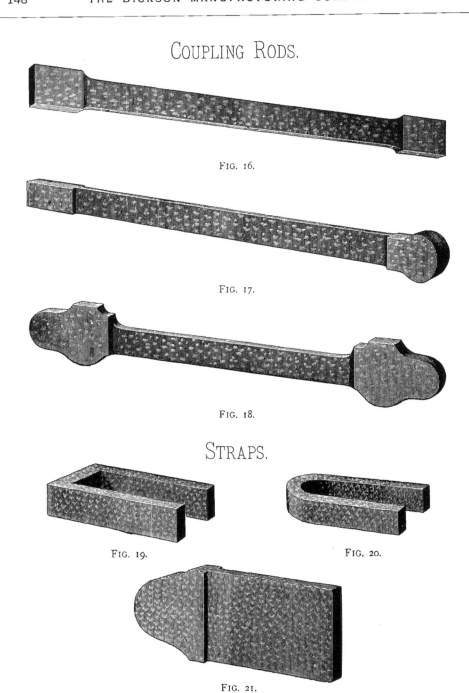

FIG. 16.

FIG. 17.

FIG. 18.

Straps.

FIG. 19.

FIG. 20.

FIG. 21.

These rods and straps are made of the best hammered iron or forged open-hearth steel, and will be furnished rough, rough finished or finished to dimensions.

Made in the USA
Charleston, SC
12 September 2013